For

Jake

'there never was a time when you or I did

not exist,

nor will there be any future when you or I

will cease to be...'

First Published in Great Britain by Kenny Barr and Sisyphus Stories

This paperback edition published in 2019 by Kenny Barr and Sisyphus Stories

www.beautifullosers.club

Copyright © 1989 by Kenny Barr

Edited and Brought to Print by Ethos Writing Agency www.ethoswriting.com

A CIP catalogue record for this book is available from the British Library
ISBN: 978-1-5272-3929-6

Cover Illustration by Tomas © 2019 Copy Made, Edinburgh

Typeset by Kelvin Carlos Typesetters

Printed and bound in Great Britain by Clays Ltd, Elcograf S.p.A.

For
Brad

Preface

For some time, I had been feeling that my life lacked direction.

Any sense of purpose.

There was certainly never going to be any chance of inspiration from within the microcosm I seemed destined to remain suffocating in.

Stifled passion, forgotten aspirations, but still content to accept and never question, and so remain.

I needed help but didn't know how to ask for it.

I craved acceptance but didn't know how to belong.

I longed to meet someone like-minded.

There can be an awkwardness around conversations involving loved ones, especially when dealing with the only real issues of life. I never liked asking my family questions on the things that troubled me, in case my thoughts might scare them, as they did me. Still do. Always will.

I wanted to save them from my rushes of panic-ridden fear, from my cries and screams caused by the stark realisation that we cannot escape from life.

We are doomed.

We have no control over our ultimate destiny.

I wanted to save them from my feelings of shear futility.

Save them from my desperation.

Save them from my visions of hopelessness.

Save them from my relentless cynicism of conventional love, with hypocritical lovers securely embraced in each other's arms but eyes clenched shut mouths tight with fear, whispering terms of endearment when really just clinging for dear life.

That love seems merely an illusion created to make the confusion bearable.

I desperately needed peace of mind.

I needed to find respite from the want of the world.

I needed some sense of euphoria. I needed to be free from the pain the knowledge of my own mortality brought.

Are these the notions of a fool? Or simply the prayers of the confused? The hurt. The lost. The lonely. The disillusioned.

We are all on the same path.

It doesn't help learning that you are not the only one. You feel that it will, but ultimately, it doesn't.

Even though, when you do find these people, some of them will be beautiful and have a lasting impression on your soul.

Andy had been away for a few months. I hardly saw him anymore as I had moved away from the old area.

He had to come home as he had a court case to attend.

When I said he'd been away, I suppose I should explain that Andy was in Greece for the summer. Working, supposedly.

Edinburgh did not hold anything for him anymore either. He had been abroad several times and the lifestyle appealed to him.

Andy, like me, did not like the idea of working his whole life, but unlike me, he occasionally suffered the indignity, until this year, when he decided enough was enough and thought he would try his luck at bumming around Crete.

Unfortunately, luck was against him.

Me, at this particular time? I was caught up in other trains of thought.

Trying to come to terms with a future that looked pretty bleak and a past that was forever hanging over me carrying a sense of impending doom.

I was feeling pretty low around this time and was making frequent trips to an old haunt for a certain kind of mental and emotional therapy.

It was at these ports of call that I would hear of Andy's exploits in Greece and began to yearn for them myself.

The big talk however, in small-town, was of Andy's impending court case and everyone's secret gloating that Andy's time in the sun was coming to an end.

I would leave these 'therapy' sessions feeling almost superior that I had not yet let my own unenviable predicament allow me to take pleasure in the misfortunes of others.

Anyway, here I was without any real direction, in a sort of self-imposed exile escaping every now and then to my picturesque places-Cramond Island and Arthur's Seat, withdrawn in self-indulgent pity.

For it is here that I find the morose natural sadness that holds a morbid source of comfort for another lost soul.

For a time, I was beginning to submit to bouts of melancholy and they were starting to take their toll.

I wanted to express a desire to be understood. Not in the company of fools. But my peers. Or somebody of like mind.

Do they exist?

Andy came home for his court appearance on the 17th of August. The Edinburgh Sheriff Court is depressing, full of the dregs of society, completely at odds with the elaborate, ornate buildings, in a contradiction of extremes.

It was a bright sunny day as I strolled up the length of the Royal Mile to see Andy appear in front of his loyal subjects. For all his trouble, he'd only collected a petty fine.

I hung around outside the actual court building, hating being inside, confined, trapped with all the forgotten elements of a disaffected society.

Andy seemed pretty pleased to see I'd turned up and he told me to hang around, with a wink, until everyone else had gone.

This was the Thursday.

He indicated for me to walk with him.

We walked and talked!

Up the Royal Mile towards Edinburgh Castle, but turning down Johnston Terrace away from it heading down by Castle Terrace.

I glanced sidelong at Andy. He was deeply tanned and looked healthy. He spoke to me excitedly about Crete and the town he was living in, Malia. 'Living like a king, having the time of his life.'

"Kenny, you'd love it there, mate. I love it!"

We continued on and turned up to our left just before The Burke and Hare bar, towards Lauriston Place.

Walking. Talking.

"Why don't you come back with me?" He was looking at me with an enthusiasm I'd never seen in him before.

On we continued.

Up past The Royal Infirmary Hospital, I glanced over and shuddered involuntarily, then around and on to George IV Bridge.

Edinburgh's beauty and majesty and historic buildings and landmarks have been written about ad nauseam. I didn't care. We didn't notice or pay attention to any of it as we walked over The Mound, with Edinburgh Castle framed to our left, The Royal Mint to our right, us in-between, and below us Princes' Street and The New Town.

We were oblivious.

Everything Andy was saying, was music to my ears. This was what I needed. My imagination was in overdrive as Andy's animation was infectious.

"But what are you doing for money? There's no way I'm working behind a bar all summer!" I said, almost indignantly.

"Do you think I would?! Me and some lads I've met are robbing apartments, we're making fortunes! Are you up for it?" Andy smiled.

I smiled back, "Too right I am!" Andy had me hooked.

I agreed to go back with him there and then.

As if by fate, but more likely through Andy's design, we were at the bottom of The Mound walking over Princes Street, just around the corner from Rose Street where Andy's Aunt Val happened to be a travel agent.

Val was a really attractive woman, in her late thirties, maybe even very early forties, but she was stunning. Blonde, tanned, very alluring.

She arranged student ID's to get us discounted travel tickets, flights and buses etc. The flight was from London to Athens, and she also booked our bus from Edinburgh to London.

Andy told her we'd come back tomorrow and pay.

As we left the shop Andy began trying to convince me to get my hair cut.

"Honest, Kenny, it will grow really quickly in the sun and because it's quite long and it's hot, you'll be glad if its shorter."

I'd let my hair grow over the summer, not consciously, more through not caring so wasn't suspicious of Andy's motives.

The following day I picked Andy up in my yellow Mini and we went up to Westburn, to see a girl named Gill we knew, to get my hair cut.

Andy kept insisting on me going really short like his, "Cos it will grow really quick in the sun..."

I told Gill just to trim it but was sure I caught Andy, from the corner of my eye, shaking his head at Gill and gesturing for her to keep cutting.

"Stop, Gill!" I barked.

She got a fright and stopped.

"Andy, I hate my hair short!"

I remembered the last time my hair had been short, I was eight years old and my dad was too preoccupied reading Titbits in the barbers until he heard me crying. I cried all the way home. I kept the hood of my Parka up for three days!

After the haircut, I left my car keys with a pal and my flat key with one of my brothers, and that was me ready to go.

We were standing in St Andrews square bus station, bags in hand, waiting to board the coach to London. I had butterflies of anticipation at what was to come but felt sad at leaving home behind.

A mutual friend, Paul, had driven us there. We shook his hand and chorused a "See you mate!"

"Take care lads," he said, awkwardly. "Have a good time, you lucky bastards."

At that moment a pretty Italian girl asked us if this was the bus to London. We winked at a jealous Paul as Andy started laying on the charm. We all had on tracksuit tops and she asked if we were football players.

Andy said we played for local club, Hibs, and introduced himself as star player John Collins, me as star player Mickey Weir, and then pointed at Paul, "And that's Alan Sneddon!" (worst player)

She laughed so we guessed she'd been in Edinburgh a while and must have seen Hibs play.

After speaking sensibly to this girl and me hoping she had a friend, Paul started to take the piss out of her and how she was dressed, but her English was good, and she recognised an insult. In her haste to escape further ridicule she attempted to jump on the bus but got trapped between the doors.

It was Paul's turn to laugh at her now. Touchy, Snoddy!

"We'd better be off now, mate." "I wish I was coming with you!"

"Aye, no luck mate," Andy feigned sincerity. "Grab that bag Kenny, that's the one my mum put the sandwiches in."

I rolled my eyes

"Right Andy," I said, "I won't forget your mummy's samiches for her wittle soldier."

We climbed on the bus and tried to smile at the Italian girl, but she sunk into her seat and turned away from us, so we winked at Paul, took our seats and forgot all about him.

"Let me sit at the window, Andy."

"Aye, ok, anywhere you want." Then sarcastically, "I'm not bothered about a window seat."

As I settled in my seat at the window Andy lit a cigarette and blew the smoke at me from the side of his mouth.

I frowned.

"Must you?!"

Andy took a deep drag and blew it at me.

"Are you going to moan at me the whole way?!"

He took another deep drag and looked like he was in deep contemplation. I turned away to look out the window and smiled to myself.

I'd known Andy since secondary school, when he was a skinhead. I knew a couple of the other skinheads who introduced me to Andy and we clicked right away.

A lot of the skinheads didn't like me, partly because I wasn't a skin, partly because I was from Sighthill and they were from neighbouring Broomhouse and the two schemes had a history of dislike, even though they were only separated by the width of the main road!

But mostly they didn't like me because I'd slept with most of their girlfriends, before them, after them, or during their relationships.

He was good looking Andy, dark hair and brown eyes with a roguish charm that women found irresistible. Always deeply tanned. Sunbeds in winter at home, sun loungers when abroad.

I'd never understood his tan orientated philosophy, but he was about to explain it to me as if reading my thoughts.

"Life's nothing without a tan mate!"

"What?!"

"Honestly Kenny, over there mate, a tan makes you. You'll see. You're not bad looking, but with a tan...."

He tailed off there, thankfully. We sat in silence.

Me, gazing out the window, reflecting on how different my life might have been if only I'd had a tan, while trying to imagine a culture I'd never experienced, and Andy, I guessed, reflecting on the one he'd left behind.

I turned to look at Andy as he began to whistle a soft tuneless whistle. One of his idiosyncrasies. I had never been able to work out why he suffered fools gladly. He was sometimes even guilty of stooping to their level. He had always been a bit of a rough diamond and I admired him for it. He was a lot cleverer than he let on, but he lacked any outward ambition, except when it came to women. He was competitive then alright, and that's when he shone.

I was beginning to regret taking the window seat as I watched Andy stretch his legs out into the aisle and smile to himself without looking directly at me.

The only compensation for me was that every time the Hostess passed Andy had to draw his legs in, and, even though he was wearing training shoes, his foot odour was still detectable!

In Andy's defence, here is his sworn testimony.

"Everybody's feet smell when you wear training shoes without socks. Arse!"

The hostess was passing us again, offering refreshments and, in an attempt to redeem himself Andy said, "I bet I get a cup of tea for nothing, watch!"

The girl came to our seat and Andy tucked his feet right under his chair. The Hostess was quite pretty, a bit too heavy on the make up for me, but Andy's type.

"Excuse me," Andy smiled up at her. "Could I have a cup of tea please?" His already white teeth gleamed even brighter against his dark tanned face.

Some loud students behind us trying to impress each other with infantile behaviour almost tripped her up as she returned with his tea.

Andy shook his head and tutted softly,

"Fuckin' students, you must get sick of them."

"Aren't you students though? That's what your tickets said?"

Andy was quick as a flash.

"Aye, but we're mature students." I swear his smile got brighter.

"I do get a little sick of them," she said.

Andy was labouring, trying to put his hands into his pockets to get his cash out.

She made an equally elaborate gesture, shaking her head, screwing up one side of her face and waving her arm in refusing payment for the tea.

Andy smiled triumphantly at me.

"You're some boy." I conceded.

He sipped away half of the tea and handed it to me.

"Cheers."

Suddenly Andy became animated.

"Kenny! Wait until we get to Greece." He couldn't contain his excitement.

"I can't wait to show you around, young gun!"

His eyes lit up and a look came over his face, half reverie, half smiling. He began whistling to himself again. Caught up once more in his own private thoughts, he lit another cigarette, and then fell silent again, reluctant to elaborate further.

I stared out the window and watched as houses and other people's lives flashed by. Faint silhouettes in countless windows, drenched in darkness, passing them as the night slipped by, leaving them behind.

"Give me a sandwich, please." I wanted to break the melancholy.

Andy opened the bag, searched through it and handed me a cheese roll.

"Tuck in Kenny. My mum made us plenty of stuff. Here, have an apple."

"No thanks. I can't eat apples unless they're peeled."

"Have some grapes then." He handed them to me as he crunched noisily into the apple.

I hate that sound! Its like nails down a blackboard to me. I didn't say anything as I knew he'd make the most of it but I'm sure he picked up on it as nobody could be that loud eating an apple.

"Kenny! What the fuck are you doing?!" Andy roared incredulously.

"Do you even peel grapes?!"

"Aye." I answered flatly.

"You're some boy, Kenny." He shook his head, then started laughing infectiously. "An arse, in fact!"

"You're the arse!" I rebuked, laughing back, continuing to peel at a grape.

Andy sipped at what was left of his free tea. He began singing in a soft whisper.

"What's that your singing?" I asked him.

"Och. It's just an old republican song," he replied.

"Why are you singing it?"

"My old boss used to sing them at work. So, I got him to teach me the words. You know I don't care about the religious songs, we're Protestants but we support Hibs who're a supposedly Catholic team. I sing both sets of football songs, I just like them, that's all."

"Sing it then."

Andy began to sing:

'It was on that dreary New Years day as the dusk of night came down. A lorry load of volunteers approached that borders town, there were men from Dublin and from Cork, Fermanagh and Tyrone, but the leader was a Limerick man Sean South from Garyowen.'

"It's good that. Sing it again and teach me the words."

Andy sang it again and again until I was sure I had learned the words.

"Right. Let me try. 'It was on that dreary New Year's Day as the dusk of night came down a bus load of...'"

That was as far as I got before Andy burst out laughing.

"A bus load?! A fuckin' lorry load, Kenny!" He chastised me.

"OK. OK. A lorry load..."

Andy mimicked me meekly. "A bus load of volunteers! Wee cowardly timid men catching their bus away to fight a war! It's a fuckin' lorry load!" He roared again with laughter. "Arse!"

I fell silent this time and was glad again that I'd taken the window seat and tried to ignore Andy's chuckling.

He resumed singing and the catchiness of the song caught my attention again.

"What's that you're mumbling, Andy?" I asked him.

Andy explained innocently, "I don't know the opening word so I just mumble it. It's either O'Reily or O'Gourly, or something O', so I just mumble 'O'Griley sent the specials in to mow the Feinians down, he thought the IRA were dead in dear old Belfast town, but he got a rude awakening with the cannon and grenade when he met the first battalion of the Belfast Brigade.'"

"That's a good one as well."

"Aye, that's one of my favourites."

With that he closed his eyes and whistled softly through his clenched teeth.

How many different ways can he whistle? I thought.

Looking at Andy, now fast asleep, and staring past him out of the window as countless houses and nameless towns floated past, I suddenly felt alone.

A strange kind of hue, an orange glow from the street lights, hung ominously over everything, its eerie spectre haunting the towns, and me.

Alone now except for my thoughts, I had time to wonder what lay ahead.

An unfamiliar country and an uncertain future. Again.

I became aware of us arriving into a city off the motorway, the outline of tall buildings and the build-up of traffic. I'd never been in London city centre before, only near it and passed by it.

We pulled in at London Victoria at about 6.30 am. The station was very cold and uninviting. The left luggage didn't open until 8.00 am, so we sat around blowing on our hands and stamping our feet until it did. Even though it was August, it was freezing.

We dropped in our bags and headed out of the station, turning left and heading towards Hyde Park, and just as we did, the sun came out.

It was Tuesday the 22nd of August 1989 and we were in London.

Like I said, I'd only ever been near London centre, once visiting a mate in Walthamstow and passed it once on the way to Woking.

A mate of a mate, Sharky, had met a girl from Slough on holiday and we had driven down to see her, but when we turned up at her work in a shopping centre, she just ignored him. We stood outside, pissing ourselves laughing, as she rebuffed him. He came out of the shop with tears in his eyes.

"Let's head to see where Paul Weller was born," I said, being the real reason I had driven us down.

I wanted to walk Oxford Street and Andy wanted to find Soho!

It was a warm morning now, and as we walked we lifted a pint of milk from a doorstep and looked in the shop windows as we drank it.

I spotted a sign for the Underground.

"Come on young gun, Let's go down the tube station!"

Andy put down the milk bottle and we started singing The Jam song together as we piled down the steps.

I stopped to call my brother, Gordon, before he went to work, to tell him we'd arrived, and we were alright.

We walked through the corridors, taking in everything. All people rushing to their destinations, each engrossed in their own worlds.

We emerged from the subway at Hyde Park. We walked on towards Marble Arch. I knew Oxford Street was nearby.

The angry rush hour traffic with horns blazing was now in full voice as we passed the car showrooms on Park Lane. Up ahead was the Marble Arch and I was struck by its size.

"Look," Andy said. "Oxford Street."

We swaggered down Oxford Street stopping for a cheeseburger and coke at a Wimpy bar and sitting listening as two barrow boys touted for custom. We lifted some fruit from them as we passed. The street was alive, much busier than Edinburgh, full of different ethnicities. I had never seen so many different types of people and styles before. All mashed together in this vibrant display of big city life. Captured by me on this warm, hazy sunny morning and committed to memory.

We finished eating and continued to walk the length of Oxford Street, taking it all in, smiling at the girls. We even got wolf-whistled from a group of girls on an open-top bus. We ended up on Pall Mall, so we walked down to Buckingham Palace then turned around and walked back up to Trafalgar Square.

It was then that we decided to take a tube. "Where?" I asked Andy.

"Anywhere."

Not far as it turned out, only to Piccadilly Circus. We sat on some fountains and rubbed our feet, with me sitting upwind from Andy.

Two philistines, sitting in the West End of London on some historical monument, rubbing our feet.

I saw a theatre sign for 'Look Back in Anger', the John Osbourne play.

"C'mon Andy lets go and see that."

"No, Kenny, let's go and see Soho!"

We really had no idea where anything was and felt pretty silly asking for directions only to be told it was 'just around the corner'.

We wandered into Soho and Chinatown about noon. It was thriving. Andy's eyes lit up at every type of sleazy attraction he could wish for.

We past Wardour street and Oxford street again and as we had already taken a tube, felt we had acted out every Jam song.

But Andy was desperate to see a 'peep' show.

This dodgy looking, greasy-haired weasel standing outside a doorway beckoned us over and led us inside. We went down some stairs and into a little dark booth. There was a slot highlighted for pound coins.

We put our coins in the slot, so to speak, got a quick flash of some-body's daughter un-sexily caressing herself, then it went black!

"Give me another pound, Kenny!"

I pulled out another two and put them in the slots.

The Vamp licked her lips in an attempt at seduction. Click. Blackness.

"Kenny!"

"No chance! This is a fuckin' con! That's 4 quid already and she's only wet her lips! It'll be a big note before we see her tits!"

The next thing I know is we are being grabbed by the scruff of the neck and dragged out the booth.

I pull myself free. "Who the fuck are you grabbing?!"

The oily-haired weasel stands in front of us.

"Aaht!" he gestures towards the door.

We laugh at him but then a curtain pulls back and two bruisers with no necks appear.

Andy nods towards them and we start backing off towards the door.

The weasel follows us up and once on the pavement roars at us.

"And don't come back you bastards!"

The whole street turns around to see what kind of people get thrown out of a peep show.

We slink off down the street complaining loudly that 'it's a rip off'.

Neon signs over doorways are all drab, broken and dirty. We were seeing Soho with fresh eyes.

A dirty seedy place selling dirty seedy sex.

Andy still loved it though. I just felt sorry for the women that worked there. The streets were even busier now.

All around us were scantily clad women. Prostitutes, transvestites or transexuals, but definitely men. This particular one was intent on catching our attention and not being very subtle about it.

He was at least six feet four inches, and that was without his high heels, under a big blonde afro wig, a boob tube showing his well-defined abs, and wearing a mini skirt, all under a full-length fur coat.

"He's looking at you, Andy."

"Fuck off!" Andy roared. "He's looking at you!"

This was the first time I could remember us debating who was getting 'the eye' from someone before.

Soho was an eye opener.

One girl dressed in skimpy shorts and a bra top flounced past us, breasts jiggling, on past a few wolf-whistling barrow boys, into a baker's shop and came out munching a mince pie!

We watched as she walked back into the shop she'd come from, walk behind the counter and take her top off.

Soho had done Andy proud.

We walked on until we came to some impressive fountains.

Andy said it was where the Scotland football supporters used to gather when they took over Wembley before International fixtures against England.

London's architecture was impressive, similar to Edinburgh but on a much grander scale.

We sat on the fountains, basking in the sunshine, eating the fruit we had lifted earlier. Andy was shaking his head as I peeled a plum before eating it.

I heard a barely audible whisper, "Arse."

We strolled back to Victoria just in time to catch a coach to Gatwick Airport.

As we hung around the departure lounge, I was feeling slightly apprehensive, as I wasn't looking forward to flying. It's not so much the flying I don't like, I told Andy, it's the crashing and dying I didn't fancy.

Andy tried to take my mind off the flight by retelling me how brilliant it was in Crete, but, after our little escapade at the peep show, he stressed the importance of not getting into trouble with the Greeks. He said they don't take any nonsense off tourists and ALL stick together in a fight.

I didn't pay him much attention as we were beginning to board our flight.

"Don't worry, Kenny," Andy assured me with a smile, "It's safer than crossing the road."

"I've never crossed the road at 450 mph."

As the queue began to narrow and we were filing down the gangway onto the plane, I was feeling uneasy. I had this sort of tunnel vision, which it was. No peripheral vision, I could only see this narrow corridor. I ignored the smile from the stewardess and edged along to our seats.

We were on a student flight, much to our dismay, and when we got to our seat, one of the three was occupied by a guy of no more than twenty years old, wearing a blue blazer and cream shorts.

Andy had the seat next to the guy but looked at me as if to say, 'no fuckin' way' and announced cheerfully indicating with his arm, "That's YOUR seat, Kenny."

I mouthed 'fuck off' as I sat down. The guy looked up and smiled pleasantly at me.

Andy nudged me in the ribs as he took his seat and whispered in my ear, "He looks like his mum dressed him!"

"They tight shorts aren't gay."

"Ooh, seems like a nice boy." Effeminately.

I hadn't brought a book to read and instantly regretted it. So, I had to content myself with reading the flight paraphernalia.

The guy with the shorts was doing the crossword puzzle in the flight booklet. I didn't have a pen and was doing the clues mentally.

I noticed he was stuck and couldn't help myself from pointing out the answer.

"That's Corporal."

"Pardon?"

"Eleven down," I repeated "Corporal."

"Oh, so it is."

"Oh, so it is." Andy, from beside me.

"And fifteen across is, Latest."

"Thanks. Here," he said, handing me the pen, "Fill in the ones you've got."

I felt Andy's elbow in my ribs.

I took the pen and booklet and with Andy on one side the and guy on the other watching me, proceeded to fill in all the remaining clues.

As we did the crossword and chatted, I hardly noticed the plane taxiing and taking off.

"What college do you go to?"

"Me?" I was surprised. "I don't go to college."

"But this is a student flight."

"Yeh I know but we don't go to college. A friend did us a favour and gave us student ID, so we could get discounted travel."

"Oh, I see. Where are you going once you get to Athens? I'm Matt by the way."

"Hi Matt, I'm Kenny and that's Andy. We're going to Crete."

"By ferry?"

"Yeh."

"Me too. Well I'm getting the ferry but actually to Corfu."

Andy leaned across me, pressing his elbow increasingly deeper into my ribcage.

"Where are you from, Matt?"

"Bristol. I'm at college there."

Every time there was a lull in the conversation, Andy leaned across me to ask Matt a question but leaned back into his own seat leaving me to listen to the reply.

We continued to make small talk until the inflight meal came.

After which, I settled back into my seat to try and rest, as I hadn't slept on the coach.

It was then that the pilot nonchalantly mentioned we were about to encounter some lightning over Italy.

That's reassuring, I thought, trying to sleep.

Surprisingly sleep did come, and I was awakened by Andy telling me that we were coming in to land.

My ears were hurting. I tried swallowing but to no avail.

Andy was talking beside me, but I couldn't hear him. All I could feel was a tremendous pressure inside my head.

Matt could see me swallowing. "Usually it helps to have something to suck on."

Andy's elbow nearly punctured my lung.

The plane touched down and I sighed with relief peeling my fingers from the arm rest.

The airport was mobbed with people. Armed police patrolled it impassively. Shoot to kill was written all over their faces as they arrogantly muscled their way through the throng of people.

Uniformed armed police in sweltering hot, brain-baking conditions can suddenly make you nervous, and our guilty consciences got the better of us as we tried to act all innocent going through customs. Even though we were.

Directly outside the airport were the taxi and bus ranks. However, they were empty.

So, we sat down on the ground along with dozens of other people. Some of them wrapped in sleeping bags, some had blankets thrown around them.

"Is public transport scarce?" I quipped. Matt had left us to find out about transport.

"It's 6.50 am now, there is a bus at 7.00 am and that takes us to the port," he told us on his return.

We moved along to the bus stop and lay against our bags. The heat and humidity were increasing and just like in the movies, the crickets cricked.

There wasn't much to see because of the heat haze, but I could still make out hillside houses, dimly lit and gleaming warmly as the morning sky changed colour.

Here I was on foreign shores under foreign skies, with no money in my pocket.

Only a notion in my heart for something else, wanting to feel something more, and carrying a forlorn hope that it existed.

'THEY'LL CALL US LONELY WHEN WE'RE REALLY JUST ALONE.'

I was starting to feel lost again.

I looked across at Andy. Did he ever feel like me?

"Kenny. Here's the bus, mate." Andy interrupted my reverie.

"So it is." I said flatly.

From the way he looked at me, I think Andy interpreted this as sarcasm. It wasn't.

We boarded the bus, and each took separate seats, across from each other, choosing to speak to each other when we felt like it, or just stare out the window.

We were just talking and looking and laughing and I hardly noticed the morning darkness totally disappear and the sunshine slip in.

It wasn't until we passed a stretch of water with some boats on it that I noticed how blue the sea was. The boats all seemed to be ultra-white, the sea a brilliant blue.

The surrounding buildings were tatty, with patchy paint stripped walls and the streets scattered with litter, but they basked in a golden yellow glow.

I got a feeling of pure optimism. One of those rare moments of elation as the early morning sunshine penetrated my being and emanated out through me.

The bus journey took an hour but felt shorter.

So. At 8.00 am, we climbed off the bus at the port of Piraeus.

The ships there were enormous. Huge, white, ocean liners.

"We'll not be on one of those. Come on, we'll go and find the ticket office and get out of this heat," Andy said, picking up his bag.

Andy was right, this heat was incredible. I hadn't noticed it until now. It was only 8.00 am and already it was in the 80's.

As I'm blond-haired and fair-skinned, I reached into my bag and brought out some sun cream, factor fifteen, and rubbed it into my face.

Andy laughed, "You, are going to fry."

Our ticket office was one hundred yards away, Matt's was further, so we arranged to meet him at a small café.

Andy went up to the desk and asked what time the ferry to Crete was. It turned out we had missed it by ten minutes! The next one wasn't until 6.30 pm! We were gutted.

We put our luggage in a storeroom and decided on what to do for ten hours.

We made our way along this bustling Athens street. The noise of the traffic was overwhelming. An intense crescendo from all the horns tooting impatiently. We barely made it across the street, without getting knocked down, to the café we had arranged to meet Matt, and ordered coffee and cheese sandwiches.

It turned out Matt's ferry was in only two hours. It wouldn't be long, he told us, until he was with his girlfriend in his friend's apartment.

We were beginning to tire of him. He then rather half-heartedly offered us his friend's address in Corfu, in case we ever 'island hop' over to see him, he said.

We eagerly accepted his invitation to visit, more to call his bluff than anything, but as his face dropped, in realisation, we then lay it on thick, especially Andy. Saying we will definitely come and see him. Andy thanked him, shaking his hand, telling him that we were hoping to island hop, but that we definitely will, now that we have somewhere to stay.

Matt started to look slightly troubled, he grabbed his luggage and said he was off to 'explore' Athens until his ferry leaves.

He shook our hands loosely, to go, and Andy sent him off with, "See you in Corfu, mate!" ringing in his ears.

Andy took a final draw on his cigarette and flicked it off in the direction Matt had just gone. Scowling, he said, "I am going to go to Corfu. In fact, I'm going to give this address to everybody we meet and tell them all that they are welcome to come and stay with me in Corfu."

We burst out laughing as Andy borrowed a pen from the waitress and wrote out several times the address in Corfu that Matt had just given us.

The sun was relentless now. Beating down on us harshly, in the hundreds.

It was too hot to go sightseeing, so I stripped down to my T-shirt and shorts and we looked around for some shade.

At the back of the ticket office was a small garden area with some trees and four benches. Three of the four were occupied. We sat down on the one free bench, tiring quickly of the heat.

We just wanted to stretch out and relax but an old Greek woman, dressed from head to toe in black, sat down next to us.

All that was visible under her headscarf was her old, brown, weather beaten face and deeply lined features. She had deep set, black, lifeless eyes.

Directly opposite a bench became free and I leapt to my feet and raced for it.

I stretched out along its entire length, face down, and made a pillow with my arms.

It felt cool in the shade.

I looked out from under my arm across at Andy and the old woman as the sun crept along the shaded area until the entire bench was exposed to the sunlight again.

A bench in the shade opposite vacated, and Andy scurried across to it but before he could get his top off to stretch out, the old woman, clearly feeling the heat too, followed him over.

Andy's face was a picture.

Then the bench he had left was snapped up.

I lifted my head up to watch as a mischievous grin snaked across Andy's face.

He began to untie the laces on his training shoes.

I watched as he stifled to contain his laughter, softly whistling through clenched teeth. He placed his trainers under the bench, closer to the old woman, then he swung his body up and around and brought his legs up onto the bench and stretched out his feet almost, but not quite, touching the old lady. He put his hands behind his head and continued his soft whistle.

I swear on all that's Holy, the old woman's nose began to twitch. She looked around herself discreetly, probably for the dead rat. Then her eyes settled on Andy's feet. She looked at him. Andy the picture of innocence.

It was now a battle of Will for her.

The intensity of the mid-day sun, or Andy's smelling feet?

No contest. The feet won.

The old woman got up to leave, shot the offending articles a withering look, and left.

Andy stretched out the whole length in victory.

"Try telling her everyone's feet smell in trainers, mate!" I yelled over.

I lay my head back down on my make-shift pillow only to be hit between the eyes with a searing bolt of sunlight. I turned my head away, but it burned into the back of my neck like a laser beam.

I tried to shield my neck by wrapping my pillow arm around it. Hopeless. I couldn't sleep in this position. I was getting more and more irritated through lack of sleep. I got up to try and walk it off.

Someone stole my bench.

I walked a few yards into what appeared to be the centre of the gardens, with a small stone fountain and a patch of concrete. People were sprawled all around. It was as if the people lying sleeping at the airport had been transported here, as they slept, and laid to rest.

I lay down against the edge of the fountain, in a tiny patch of shade, and curled my body around the cold concrete.

My residency at the fountain was short lived. The sun struck again. I opened my eyes, which were sore from the intense light, and saw Andy, less than thirty yards away, sound asleep on his now shaded bench.

I got up and walked wearily over to him.

"Andy." I shook him. "I can't sleep. The sun keeps hitting my face. Move over and let me on."

"What?" Andy growled. "What is it?!"

"Move over and let me on the bench," I repeated

Andy made a real meal of moving to give me space.

I squeezed myself in to the small strip of room he made available and was thankful just to be in the shade.

I closed my eyes to sleep at last but heard Andy in a whining mimicking voice.

"Move over. The sun's shining in my face. I can't sleep. Oh, the sun. It's killing me. I'm dying in this heat. It's like an oven! Some traveller!"

I still couldn't get comfortable. So, I got up again.

"Oh, for fuck sake, where are you goin' now?!" Andy yelled after me. "Fuckin' arse," he muttered as he settled back down.

Not far from the benches were some trees. Their branches seemingly slumped over from the heat, but beneath them, a patch of shaded ground called out invitingly.

I dropped down exhausted, and spread-eagled myself out, enjoying the cool ground underneath. I could still feel the heat all around but now it covered me in a weightless blanket and I drifted off to sleep.

"Kenny. Come on. Wake up."

I awoke, startled, and a little disorientated, to find Andy standing over me. All I could make out was his silhouette as the glare of the sun was behind him.

I sat up and rubbed at my eyes to try and clear my head. I was hungry. My stomach was grumbling. My head was splitting, and the crickets seemed to be reaching a crescendo. I wished it would all fucking stop.

Andy helped me to my feet.

"Come on, we'll get something to eat," he said.

"Let's stop at the ticket office first so I can get my sunglasses." I was still rubbing my eyes.

The ticket office was busier than before and this time the guy let us go into the storeroom unaccompanied. We looked at each other. Was he really this trusting?

I told Andy to go to my bag and get my sunglasses, while I went to the most expensive looking bags and rifled through the side compartments. I pulled out a pair of Ray Bans and put them on my head. Grabbed a roll of notes, and a camera. That was all, as I heard Andy cough.

I made my way back to the exit just as the guard walked in.

"Got them." I pointed up to my glasses and put them over my eyes.

"Ella, ella," the guard called impatiently.

We walked out with him as if he had escorted us the whole time and walked back out into the not quite so bright sunshine thanks to my new Wayfarers.

"What did you get?" Andy asked, as we made our way to a café at the back of the ticket office.

The café was a huge glass structure but cool and clean inside.

I began counting the roll. "12,000 Drachma, this camera and obviously the shades."

Andy smiled. "£45, nice one Kenny."

We ordered two cheese toasties and two cokes.

After we'd finished eating, we took a walk around and sat at the edge of the water looking around the port as it opened out to sea.

I imagined the Greek heroes of the past, Odysseus, and Alexander the Great especially, sailing this sea. I thought of their great myths and exploits and kept thinking of Alexander's line, 'it is a lovely thing to live with courage and die leaving an everlasting flame'. I felt small in comparison, humbled by their legends.

Kicking my heels against the harbour walls I wanted to say something profound. I just sighed involuntarily and kept staring out across the alluring expanse of the Mediterranean.

Andy tapped my leg. "Come on. We'll get some film for that camera."

We bought the film and took some Montgomery Clift type pictures. With us posing, in turns, sensitive, pensive, all angst and longing. Looking thoughtful, a hint of futility, a gesture of futility in our eyes.

Looking at Andy acting like that, lending the photos meaning, maybe he did sometimes feel like me.

He must have had something in his mind if he knew how to look like that.

It was time for the ferry. Andy was wrong. We were on one of those gigantic ships.

As we were climbing the gangway we were told to keep to the top deck. People were scrambling past us, trying to get a cabin as it turned out.

Seeing as it was still warm, we didn't bother and sat up on deck, with our feet up on the rails looking out across the sea.

The sky was turning a wonderful pale, yellow colour, with the sun in the centre, radiating a magnificent golden glow. It was shining on us. Reflecting off the water, stretching away to a seamless eternal horizon. A cooling breeze whispered over us. I felt alive, free, and knew that this, was the beginning of something special.

'ON A BLUER OCEAN AGAINST TOMORROWS SKY'

Little did I know the ferry took twelve hours!

We were told that we could store our bags down in the bowels of the ship. The ship went down for several levels and once again we were faced with rows and rows of unattended bags! Picking out the expensive ones and quickly and quietly emptying the contents. It's important never to be greedy in a situation like this, accept the opportunity presented but don't risk getting caught with only one escape route, overboard.

The ship's levels ranged in class from A to D. We were in D.

Up on deck it was now lovely and cool. The sun was still shining brightly, shimmering off the water, but had lost its intensity.

The coast of Athens was barely perceptible as I stared down into the wash. I began to get butterflies.

Andy was pretty quiet. He was acting like he had something on his mind, but he wasn't sharing it with me. He was looking into the wash also and chewing his lip slightly.

We decided to go to the bar area and Andy was delighted to discover that the beer was only 50 drachs, about 25p per can. I got three. Two for Andy and one for me and then we wandered around.

It was a pretty big room. Noisy. Filled with different nationalities. A couple of TV's were on, showing English programmes dubbed into Greek.

An announcement was made over the address system about a ticket check as someone had sneaked on.

I moaned out loud about no seats available and a girl smiled at my comment, so I asked her if she was English.

She said she was and introduce herself as Ellen. She was very pretty, from London, and very self-assured, cocky. She introduced her friend as Ann-Marie. She had a pretty face, was plumpish, a bit tarty, and from Birmingham.

Andy began flirting immediately with Ellen, directing all his attention towards her and I knew he'd earmarked Ann-Marie for me.

Ellen behaved like she came from money. Very confident and slightly aloof.

We smiled and introduced ourselves, sitting down.

They asked if we had a cabin and when we replied we hadn't, they offered to let us share with them, as two dirty old men had been pestering them. Me and Andy exchanged a glance which Ellen picked up on, and the game was afoot!

Ellen then crossed her legs, deliberately showing a bit of thigh. Ann-Marie sat up pushing her breasts up, she couldn't help but expose her thighs.

Ann-Marie would have gladly taken any one of us, but we both wanted Ellen, and Ellen knew it. So, she flirted with both of us.

I soon tired of her three-way interplay, and focused all my attention on Ann-Marie, who was looking a little left out. This seemed to bother Ellen and I guessed she probably did this a lot.

As the drinks warmed me, Ann-Marie's ample assets looked all the more inviting and she had a pretty face and kind eyes. She also looked delighted that I was making an effort with her and ignoring her better-looking pal.

I was in like Flynn.

Ellen had now cooled a bit towards Andy and was attempting to win my attention back, but I ever so slightly turned my chair away from her.

Ann-Marie perked up with pride and her breasts ripened before my eyes.

The alcohol was flowing and the conversation easy and open, when they suddenly announced they were going to their cabin, and if we came with them, they could show us where it was.

We drained our cans and got up to leave with them. Andy nudged me in the ribs as he linked arms with Ellen.

The cabins were in sets of four, with twin bunks, and we had this one to ourselves. So much for the mad rush to find cabins.

The girls said they were going to the toilet. We let them go first then went out quickly behind them.

We checked our hair in the mirror and washed our dicks in the sink laughing.

We got back to the cabin just as they returned.

As if on cue Ellen sat down on the bottom bunk next to Andy and Ann- Marie began to climb up on to the top bunk. I reached out and put my hands on her ample bottom and gently pushed her up onto the bunk, she giggled provocatively. Music to my ears.

Andy was already stretched out and wrapped around Ellen, before Ann-Marie had settled. I was barely on the bunk before she started kissing me, sticking her tongue deep into my mouth. Ah, that sweet taste of alcohol on her breath.

I released her heavy breasts from her bra and massaged them gently, tracing my fingers over her large erect nipples as she stifled her moans.

Our hands were all over each other. Hers rubbing me stiff, me stroking her wet.

When I tried to enter her, she whispered that she couldn't, not with her pal lying underneath.

"Let's go up onto the deck then?"

"No, I can't."

We continued to pet heavily working each other up until I finally got relief, all over her charms.

I couldn't hear much noise coming from bellow so guessed Andy had met the same excuse.

We continued to pet for most of the night, until we drifted off to sleep, spent, again.

The girls were up before us in the morning, and I suppose slightly embarrassed. They had dressed and were ready to go before they woke us.

We said our goodbyes, hurriedly, with a peck on the cheek from them both. Ellen let her lips brush my neck as she pulled across me. One-upmanship on her pal to the end.

Andy said we might bump into them in Crete and gave them Matt's address in Corfu, in case they island hopped.

"I doubt it," Ellen said sarcastically.

"You never know," Andy said. "Where are you going?"

"Malia!" They chorused.

We tried to keep our faces straight until they left.

"How did you get on?" Andy asked, putting on his top.

"Hand job." I said flatly, "What about you?"

"Same."

"What does that say about us, Andy?"

"What do you mean?"

"Two wanks!"

The port at Heraklion was hectic. Hustle and bustle and noise. Everybody was trying to get off the boat at the same time. Some trying to locate loved ones, some just rude and obnoxious. There were hundreds of bodies pushing and jostling and the taxi rank was about survival of the fittest.

We played their game and began barging our way arrogantly through the throngs of people and just jumped into a taxi. It was already taken with an English couple who just happened to be going to Malia. Andy thanked them for letting us share and gave them Matt's address in Corfu if they ever island hopped.

We struck up a casual conversation. Well, Andy did. I like to switch off in moments like this whereas Andy excels at small talk and these situations. I admired his charm.

He did, however, punctuate his conversations with sly digs in my ribs when the man said something he didn't agree with. Andy had a great way of still smiling at someone and nodding his head in agreement, whilst his eyes conveyed something else.

I didn't mind appearing anti-social and continued to look out the window into the darkness as my melancholy imagination ran riot trying to get inside the lives of the people inside the houses whose lights glowed distantly on the surrounding hills.

I put my hand up to the window to shield the reflecting light from within the taxi, so I could take in more.

All I could make out now were sparsely branched trees casting eerie shadows.

I hate myself for dwelling on these nightmare scenarios, thinking all kinds of morbid eventualities.

I used to do it, to make me feel more alive, as if reminding myself to take the most out of every experience or suffer the consequences of a life untouched or unmoved by anyone gone before me. I didn't want to feel that they had lived in vain. Now though, these thoughts haunt me at will.

Thankfully, the taxi journey was only about forty-five minutes long.

'TOUCH ME WHEN THE SUN COMES UP AND TELL ME THAT WE'RE HOME'

We arrived in Malia between 6-7 am.

The driver pulled into the taxi rank which was located on our right-hand side, and we all made to get out, splitting the fare.

The couple asked if we had anywhere to stay. I looked at Andy as he told them we did. We thanked them and said goodbye. They walked off.

As we stood there, the first thing that struck me was the smell. That faint oil smell that I had detected in the air at the Airport. Greece.

The sky was just beginning to lighten. The cold night blue softening ever paler. We stood there now with our bags, lonesome travellers.

I looked up and down the length of the street and over to a road directly opposite us.

"This is the Main road," Andy said as he pointed. "That's the Beach road down there."

We picked up the bags and walked as if heading out of town in the opposite direction. I saw a sign saying Knossos.

"C'mon. Let's find Ian."

I followed Andy along the main street. I gazed into the various shop windows as we passed but couldn't make out what they were.

"Up here," Andy said turning right. Then left. It all seemed like a maze to me, but which Andy manoeuvred expertly.

Although it was barely 7 am, old Greek women, dressed from head to toe in black, sat outside their houses, nodding politely as you passed them.

"Why are they all dressed in black, Andy?"

"Ninjas, Kenny," he said secretly, from the corner of his mouth as he continued walking.

And that was what they came to be called. You would see them at any time of day or night. 6 am, 7 am. 9 pm, 10 pm, 3 am, 4 am.

I never passed through the old town without seeing them, either on the steps or more spookily at the windows, peering out.

Custodians of the old town? Or eerie reminders of lost youth?

The more you became aware of them, the more they seemed to appear. Lining your way. Sometimes it was hard not to look into their watery benevolent eyes. The eyes only the old have.

I once saw an old man sitting at the back corner of a bus and he had the saddest old eyes I'd ever seen. It was the only time I could have cried for somebody I didn't know. I don't know what I saw in those eyes that day except that they moved me enough to say.

"Spies." Andy opined.

"Eh?!"

"Spies. The ninjas. They're like the eyes of the village."

'BECAUSE THE PEOPLE IN THE VILLAGE KNOW IT DOESN'T MATTER WHERE YOU CHOOSE TO GO THE ENDS THE SAME'

"How far now?" I asked. Thinking Andy was lost.

We were passing an apartment block as I said this and a guy sleeping outside on the ground floor balcony on a Lilo looked up at us. We must have looked suspicious to him. Talking over loudly and trying to find the apartment 'this way'.

"Do you want something, pal?!" I aimed at him. He shot back down out of sight.

The apartment we stopped outside, white with blue piping, looked familiar to me.

"Kenny. I don't think Ian's here," Andy admitted, dropping his bag. "I thought we'd passed here before."

"This is the block, but it doesn't look like he's here. He was staying here with a girl." He said this whilst gently tapping on the door.

"Andy, knock louder than that!" I said banging on the window.

Andy sighed, and shook his head ever so slightly.

"That's the apartment next door, Arse..."

"Ian!" Andy shouted, still rapping the door. He gave up and came over to where I was sitting on my bag.

"He's not here," he announced.

My turn to sigh. "Where would he have gone?"

Andy didn't have time to answer. A girl appeared at the window I'd been knocking on.

"What's going on?" she asked.

"We're looking for a mate!" I said sharply.

"What mate?!" she asked suspiciously.

"What the fu..."

Andy put his hand across my mouth. "I used to live here with my pal, but I had to go home for a few days..."

"Oh hiya," her voice softened as she recognised Andy. "He's not here anymore. He left with that girl."

"Do you know where they went?" Andy asked, hopefully.

"No. They didn't say."

"Oh, ok..."

Andy was about to continue talking but she smiled and shut the window. Andy caught me staring at him.

"C'mon. Tim and that live just over that way. We'll go and see them."

We hauled our bags up onto our shoulders and Andy proceeded to lead me through the old town streets once more.

We passed the guy on the Lilo on the balcony again, he bobbed his head up to take a look.

"You're like a fuckin' Jack in the Box!" Andy scolded him. "Put your head down you, nosey prick!"

It was good to see Andy angry. He could handle himself Andy. He was an early football casual, but too often for my liking, he pacified people. The guy's head shot down. Am sure Andy wanted to chant 'CCS'!

It was only a short distance between the two apartments, but my patience was wearing thin.

Andy entered the hallway of an apartment block and stopped at the first door on his right, knocking loudly this time.

A guy with brown, shoulder length hair, answered the door with a grunt.

"Hi Jools, is Tim there, mate?"

He grunted again, "Wait there," closing the door on us.

Andy didn't have to look at me to know what I was thinking. He was leaning against the door frame looking down, chewing his lip.

The door opened again and a guy with blond, shorter hair answered the door sleepily, "Alright Andy?" I detected a faint Glaswegian sounding accent.

"Tim, have you seen Ian?" Andy asked hopefully.

"He moved back to Hersonisos, mate". Tim had a definite Glaswegian accent.

I leaned back against the wall and listened to Andy drop hints about us having nowhere to stay.

"I've just came back after my Mobbing and Rioting court case mate, and Ian's pissed off from our apartment."

Deaf ears.

"I just know that he's back in Hersonisos." Tim repeated.

It was obvious we weren't getting an invitation in.

We stood there for a few moments with Tim gradually closing the door more and more with a meek smile until it shut.

Andy picked up his bag and walked past me. I picked up mine which was getting heavier and traipsed after him.

"Who were they, Andy?"

"That was Tim and Julian, that I've been telling you about."

"Oh aye, your mates over here. Some mates."

"I can't believe they never let us in!" Andy was shaking his head.

"Why don't we just go back up there, and punch fuck out of them?!"

Andy was contemplating it, "We'll find a place to put our bags and go back up later."

Too weary to argue the point, we trudged on. It was still before 7 am but I could feel the impending heat.

Reaching the taxi rank, we threw off our bags and slumped down dejectedly on the steps of the doorway to the taxi office.

Andy reached into his pockets for his cigarettes. I reached into mine and pulled out my last £20 note in English money and a few thousand Drachma.

"Fuckin' brilliant Andy. Three days travelling, tired, dirty, hungry and skint and nowhere to stay! What the fuck am I doing here? Why did I let you talk me into this?!"

"There's no point in moaning now, Kenny."

The penny dropped.

"You knew he wouldn't be here. Didn't you? That's why you wanted me to come back with you? Isn't it?"

"I didn't KNOW he wouldn't be here," Andy admitted. "But I did have an idea."

"Oh, an idea?" I sat shaking my head in disbelief. "Any IDEA, what to do now?"

Andy drew on his cigarette and looked out into the street. "Nah."

We sat in silence. Andy drawing thoughtfully on his cigarette, hands up at his face, resting against his knees.

I sat with my legs stretched out and my head leaning back against the doorway entrance.

"We'll be alright, Kenny."

I heard Andy's voice from a million miles away.

I sat there feeling slightly unreal. Trying to comprehend what being stranded all these miles from home meant. I had a feeling that it was bad, but might not be, hoping against hope.

We heard footsteps approaching and looked up to see the couple we'd shared the taxi with.

"Haven't you got anywhere to stay? We've found a Hotel up in the village called 'Sweet Dreams' it's only 3000 drachs."

3000 was about half of what we had. So, we picked up our bags of cement and followed them back up into the village.

'Sweet Dreams' was just a little further up into the old town than Andy's last apartment. The couple told the owner, Dimitri, that they knew us, and he gave us a key as we handed over the 3000.

We climbed the stairs to our first-floor room, and the couple went to the room opposite. We thanked them for coming to find us. Andy opened the door and we flopped down on our beds inhaling the fresh sheets.

I remember Andy waking me up. I don't know how long I'd slept for, but I felt good.

Brilliant sunshine streamed through the window. We shaved, showered and dressed feeling replenished.

"We'll go and see Tim and that now," Andy said, with real intent, tying the waist of his shorts. "Then I'll show you around." He sounded invigorated.

Walking around the village in daytime was almost magical. Gone was the eerie haunted feel.

People were milling around. Going into, what I could now see, were different types of shops, but at night looked vacant.

I was amazed at the blueness of the sky and the lightness of the scene. It was like my first real glimpse of Greece in the sun at Athens.

A brilliant clearness. A dazzling brightness and I didn't want to wear sunglasses. Feeling somehow that they would dull my vision. Lessen the clarity. I wanted to take everything in.

The heat was intense as we made our way along the narrow uneven pavements. Almost all the houses were painted white with pastel coloured shutters and the windows flung wide open to welcome in the light.

We made our way up to the apartment we had visited, what seemed ages ago, passing the odd black clad women who no longer appeared sinister. Andy banged on the door.

The door opened, and we were invited in by Tim. "Sorry about earlier lads, we were a bit shocked at the knocking."

Andy visibly eased. Tim introduced himself to me and his cousin Dominic and pointed over to Julian, who was putting his shoes on.

Tim and Dom were cousins from Glasgow, Julian was from Oldham, near Manchester.

We sat down on their beds and exchanged small talk.

Tim spoke the most. Julian was arrogant and left soon after we arrived, mumbling, "See ya."

We talked about Ian going away, us going to try and find him but mostly about Andy's court case.

Finally, Andy mentioned that we were broke.

Tim said he had something arranged and we should meet tonight at 11.30 pm at The London Pub.

We left the apartment feeling relieved and headed down to the Main road to catch a bus through to Hersonisos.

The Main road was a different proposition in the daytime. Cars, but mostly bikes, roared their way around. Revving their engines and blasting their horns.

Every shop was bursting with people. Holiday makers and locals alike. We stopped at a fruit stand to get some change and Andy impressed me with the Greek he knew, I didn't know at the time, but he was just repeating the same words. Then though, it sounded impressive.

Andy strolled along that street like a native. Nodding and waving to people like the Prodigal son returning from his court victory.

I thought he must be pretend waving at everyone but a few people on bikes tooted and waved and shouted over, asking when he got back.

He was in his element.

"That's the Beach Road down there," he pointed at the only opening. "That's the real Malia. It's about a mile long with all the good bars and clubs on it. We'll see it tonight."

I looked along the street we had came from, trying to remember the opening and get my bearings.

The bus arrived, and we got on.

It drove back out the way we had entered the night before. Only this time, I could see properly, what had only been shadowy outlines, the previous night.

Andy spoke to me the whole time. Pointing out various places.

The Kalia Bar, about half a mile out of town on our left-hand side, an all- night bar that the Greeks and workers frequented after work, but not tourists.

For a quiet drink, he pointed down a road to our right that ran parallel with the road we were on, that was the Stalis Road.

Hersonisos wasn't all that far away, between four and seven miles, I estimated. There was some impressive scenery on route. A long golden

lager louts. I sipped at my coke as Andy downed a few beers in quick succession.

Tim arrived bang on 11.30 pm. The street didn't look like it could hold any more people. It was loud, from the music blasting out of pub speakers, to groups of men and women screeching at each other. Drunk, contorted faces.

We waited until Andy drained his glass then headed back up the Beach road into the old town.

I enjoyed the quiet.

Tim said he had an apartment lined up, but I recognised the apartment of the guy on the Lilo and decided to do that.

When we got closer to the apartment, I noticed Andy shifting nervously on his feet. He quickly offered to keep look-out.

Tim and me, climbed over the balcony and tried the doors. Locked. I noticed they also opened in the way, which meant you couldn't just pull them open. Kicking them in would mean too much noise, so we dropped down below eye level to the height of the handle and began picking at the wooden beading around the glass planes. Tim produced a small screwdriver and began levering them off.

As they were only secured with a couple of thin nails, they cracked off easily, but every crack sounded like a small gunshot to us.

The glass fell silently into our eagerly outstretched palms and I noticed that they didn't use putty on their glass.

Tim reached his hand through the gap and I heard the sweet click of the lock opening. We smiled at each other as Tim slipped inside and I remained on the balcony to reattach the beading.

A short time passed them Tim reappeared and we silently creeped over the balcony and edged down the street. I held Tim back, and said to go quietly, to see if we could sneak up on Andy to see if he was keeping look-out for us.

We got to the spot where Andy had been when we left him. No Andy. Another few hundred yards and we could just about see him. No good to us.

We walked down towards him. Andy instinctively looked up and he gleefully approached us, quickening his step to shorten the distance from where he was, to where he should have been.

We doubled back on ourselves to Tim's apartment.

As we were about to divide the money between the three of us, there was £150 in English money and £300 in travellers' cheques, Tim asked about Dom's share.

"What share?" I asked. "Is he here? Only people that take the same risks as me, mate, are entitled to a share."

Tim saw my logic, "Fair enough."

We took £50 each and Tim put the cheques in a pair of dirty socks and threw them under his bed.

"Beach road to celebrate?" Andy looked at me.

It felt good to have money in my pocket. That morning's feeling of desperation had dissipated.

Standing on the Beach road with a bottle of beer in my hand, I felt elated.

Walking up the Beach road later that night we bumped into two girls. Obviously drunk from the way they were staggering. I stopped to talk to them, but Tim and Andy just stepped in front of me and took one each.

They both started kissing them and I was left standing there slightly bemused. When they all began walking up into the old town, I simply followed behind shaking my head.

Tim led his girl into a building under construction. Andy pulled at his and included me as if to initiate a threesome. She was undecided, and it might have taken some persuasion from Andy, but she was too drunk to find attractive. She wasn't provocative, rather stupid drunk, wearing that gargoyle expression of the worse for wear, that swung it. I held back and let Andy lead her next to Tim's building site, where he lay her down on some slabs of concrete and had sex with her. Her loud moans of enjoyment brought some Ninjas to their windows, but they quickly disappeared just as Tim reappeared, fixing his trousers.

It was comical watching Andy's girl trying to maintain her dignity in front of us while obviously fuelled by her desire to have him. Lust won, as she wriggled her way from underneath him to place herself on top.

I walked on with Tim who totally ignored the girl he'd just been with.

She was adjusting her clothes and telling her mate to hurry up!

"In a minute" she muttered, over and over.

Andy's minute was finally up, and he caught up with us. We arranged to meet Tim the following morning, early, and said goodnight.

"Twice, in one-night young gun?" I said.

"Told you it was easy over here, mate."

"Aye, I noticed. Is that how it works? Just cutting in? Every man for himself?"

Andy didn't reply. He was ultra-competitive when it came to women.

We got up early the next day and dressed in T-shirts, shorts, sunglasses and bum-bags, the proper tourist look, and went downstairs and paid for another two days.

We then walked along to hire a motorbike. The bike shop belonged to a guy called Alex. Andy knew him quite well, so he gave us a good deal on a bike. A Guillera 250. Andy was delighted.

A 125 would have been good enough but when Andy had money, he had to have a big bike. Another good thing about a big bike he told me was that you could get three people on it. So true to his word, we went along to pick up Tim.

Tim was ready for us coming. He had been practising the signatures on the traveller's cheques and had them down to a tee. He was excellent at signing signatures.

The three of us drove to Stalis, and Andy was right, a bigger bike took three people comfortably.

Me and Tim got off the bike to enter the first exchange and Andy shot off up the road to wait for us. We looked at each other and I pretended to squint my eyes to see where Andy was.

"Do you think he's a safe enough distance away?!"

Tim laughed and climbed the few steps into the exchange office.

"Hello, can I cash some travellers' cheques please?" he asked, confidently approaching the desk.

"Certainly, my friend, how much?" said the guy at the desk.

"£100 please."

"Yes, yes. Sit down please."

I became wary at him asking Tim to sit. I thought he was trying to stall us. Tim sensed my tension and pulled me away to look at the posters on the wall advertising excursions. "Look there's a boat trip," he said brightly. "Relax," he then whispered to me under his breath.

Tim sat down at the desk and opened up his bum-bag removing two cheques, "Do you have a leaflet on those boat trips please?" he pointed casually at the wall, picked up a pen and began to sign both cheques and in one motion handed them over. I was impressed with Tim's calmness.

The guy reached in to a drawer and I tensed, he pulled out a calculator. He punched in some digits. Then he opened another drawer and pulled out a thick wad of notes. He counted out the Greek equivalent and handed it over to Tim with a smile, picking up the travellers' cheques and not even asking for ID or bothering to look at the signatures!

I'll never forget the thrill of roaring along on the motorbike to the next shop with the sun on or backs and time on our side. An almost ethereal feeling, perhaps caused by the heat haze, of otherworldliness, of almost being withdrawn and able to see yourself from above. As if knowing that one day you would look back and reflect on it like this. Taking part in something but knowing it's going to be all right. Marking your time as these events shape your life, knowing that the years will pass, and you will be richer from the experience.

I can't express enough, that feeling from the sun. The warmth that permeates the air, it surrounds you, it engulfs you.

Not in the obvious way. Everyone can appreciate the heat from the sun, but that sense of well-being that it generated.

And to me, to all of us, its glow gave us protection.

I had the sense of being ensconced in a warm blanket of protection. We were open to it, dressed lightly in T-shirts and shorts, and it glowed on us. We weren't having to fight against the cold adverse weather conditions of home. We were burning brightly in this picture of life, under the clearest sky I'd ever seen, and I'd never been so vibrant and alive.

It was still only noon, so we headed back to Malia. We drove down the Beach road and stopped a quarter of the way down on the left-hand side and went in to one of the more exclusive Hotels to use their swimming pool. We had to pay 800 drachs each, but it was worth it. The price included your sunbed and it was an older cliental. We didn't want to flaunt our money or be seen too often with our peer group, also it was so much more peaceful.

Tim's cousin Dominic, Dom, was there with Julian. We stripped off our T- shirts and shorts, and me and Andy raised a few eyebrows as we were wearing identical black speedo trunks with a green logo.

Andy hastily explained that we had stolen them from Macro the day before we left.

There were two other guys there, another blond-haired lad called Tim, he was a hairdresser from somewhere in England and Lloyd, a Brummie guy, with a big nose, who loved himself. He turned out to be alright. Maybe Dave was there.

We all mucked about in the pool, talked about our football teams. Me and Andy Hibs, Tim and Dom, Celtic. Julian was from Oldham, but he supported Manchester city, and Hibs had just signed the Oldham goalkeeper, Andy Goram.

The banter was good natured but there was a slight attempt from people to exert their dominance, which is common amongst young men, especially from different parts of the same city, let alone different parts of the country.

Tim 2, being a hairdresser, started talking about going bald and we all held our hairlines back for inspection, so Tim could assess us. He mentioned that Julian's hairline was quite high, and I saw again Julian's arrogance.

He replied in his thick Manc accent that 'it always 'ad been and anyway he didn't give a fuck if he went bald, cos he'd still be good-lookin'.

We lay around the pool sunbathing and generally laughing and joking, except when Tim kept trying to get people into the pool when it suited him, and Julian telling him to 'quit mithering me'.

I suppose I was still an unknown quantity as I didn't get asked and was kept out of the gentle ribbing between them. I was glad as it gave me a chance to assess their capabilities.

Andy was getting bored and still desperate to show me around, so we left them at the pool and climbed on the bike. Andy loved pulling the big Guillera off the stand and cranking up the engine.

He told me how beautiful the hills surrounding Malia were and popped a wheelie in his excitement to be off. He revelled in the gazes from impressed females as we shot off down the Beach road.

Andy turned left then raced up to the top of the road next to Galaxy bar and roared along the main road to our right.

I looked over and down to my right to acknowledge Stalis, then to my left as we passed The Kalia bar. I hadn't been there yet, but I was beginning to recognise places Andy had previously pointed out and where roads led to other roads rather than the direct routes.

We drove on for about a mile until the road took a wide bend to the right. We turned off left at the signpost for Mohos.

The road snaked and twisted upwards. Driving up the weaving mountain roads reminded me of the opening to the film, The Italian Job, and I could hear Matt Monroe's refrain 'on days like these' in my head as the road wound and the scenery flashed by.

The road grew steeper and Andy kept dropping gears to climb it, until the road flattened out. Andy pulled the bike in. The road seemed to rise another level and continue on, but he stopped here.

I dismounted and Andy put the bike on its stand.

"Look, Kenny." He pointed. "It's amazing up here."

It wasn't quite the fantastic spectacle I was expecting from his build up, but it was impressive. I looked down to the coastline and couldn't tell where the sea met the sky, there were only shades of blue. A twisting sandy shoreline and the whites of the buildings that constituted Stalis blending into Malia. Far away to our left Hersonisos was perceptible. The heat and the noise from the crickets seemed to intensify the view.

I asked Andy what was behind the bend where the road continued, and he said that he didn't know, he'd never gone that far.

It was hard to believe that just twenty-four hours earlier I had been sitting on a pavement with nothing, and here I was now, sitting on top of the world, master of all I surveyed.

We sat on some rocks and marvelled at it all. The beginning of a fantastic adventure.

'IN THE EVENT THAT THIS FANTASTIC VOYAGE SHOULD TURN TO EROSION AND WE NEVER GET OLD'

We drove back in silence, and as we descended, each level bought us back down to earth with it. I wasn't thinking quite so grandly as before, much more even minded now and less loftily.

It must have been between 5-6 pm as you could detect a slight change in temperature. We stopped at a supermarket, and Andy bought the only things I ever saw him eat in Crete.

Two rolls, a packet of ringed, pizza flavour crisps and a carton of Milko, chocolate flavoured milk.

We took them back to the apartment to eat and fell asleep reading the newspapers.

Andy woke me. It was 10.30 pm. We showered and dressed, then drove through to Hersonosos to a bar called The Star bar, where Ian worked.

A few drinks later I got talking to a red-head nurse at the bar, called Fiona. She was from Edinburgh. It turned out she lived in the same area near me at The Pleasance. I told her we could have met at the 'Argyle' and saved ourselves a few quid.

Anyway, I left them, and went with her back to her apartment, keen to score again on my second night. I told Andy I'd see him back here later and he winked as we left arm in arm.

Fiona climbed the three flights of tight stairs to her apartment block and I rubbed her bottom the whole way up. She was giggling but telling me to be quiet as her flat-mate was asleep inside. She led me outside onto the balcony and we started kissing and groping each other passionately. I was erect, but it was uncomfortable as I needed to pee.

I pulled myself out of her grasp and told her I needed the toilet, so I crept through the balcony doors as quietly as I could into the apartment and headed over to a half open door that I hoped was the toilet. I heard her pal sigh loudly, she was asleep, in the living room on the couch in just her underwear. I tripped over something causing her to sigh again.

I was standing over the toilet bowl trying to piss with a hard-on. The piss was flying everywhere. I was trying to push the stream down and aim into the bowl but pissed up the cistern, I tried to piss in the sink but pissed up the vanity mirror. I decided to piss in the shower. I was squeezing my piss out as forcefully as I could incase Fiona walked in and caught me pissing in her shower with an erection whilst her semi-naked pal lay next door and thought I was a pervert. The bathroom was a piss-soaked mess. I wiped myself on a towel, her mates, hopefully, and crept back to the balcony but only managed to kick something over.

"For fuck sake!" her pal moaned.

Please be her towel.

I was expecting Fiona to have adjusted her clothing when I got back but her breasts were still hanging out as I'd left them. I took up where I left of, rubbing her all over. We sank down onto a sun lounger. It was a bit awkward.

So, we stood up against the balcony, she slipped out of her dress and I saw her pale white flesh shining in the moonlight, I eased my boxers down. She reached down and grabbed and pulled at me, trying to get me inside her. I pushed her ever so slightly and she took a tumble almost over the balcony.

"It's too awkward like this. Take me from behind," she panted.

I turned around to face the other way.

"This is even more awkward!"

When I half turned around to face her, I could see that in the throes of passion, humour was lost, she was puzzled and unsure.

Ok Fiona, just as you asked. I entered her from behind.

There I was, screwing a nurse over her balcony on my second night in Crete. I had a pocket full of money, a girl on my dick and the biggest smile on my face.

When I finally turned up at the Star bar to meet Andy, I still had a smile on my face.

"No need to ask how you got on."

"Ask away, young gun," I said.

Andy smiled, "Are you ready to go home?"

I nodded. Drunk still but fulfilled.

Andy gunned the bike back through to Malia, huddled over the handle bars, full throttle.

"This is why I get a big bike, Kenny!" he shouted over the noise of the engine.

I must admit it was electrifying.

Roaring along the road in the dead of night, just the moonlight reflecting off the water to our left, racing to get home.

The next day was Saturday. Derby day back home. Hibs versus Hearts for us. Rangers v Celtic for Tim and Dom.

We were eating breakfast together and guessing what the results would be. Tim mentioned that he wanted to split the money with his cousin, Dom.

I said no way. The only way anybody got a share was if they took part. They said that no matter what, they had always split it before.

I explained that it didn't matter to me what had happened before. I didn't risk my neck getting caught, just to give a share to someone's cousin. So, from now on we all did it together. Andy agreed with me and so did Tim. Dom said, 'fair enough,' and we went back to discussing the football and talking about their previous 'missions', as they liked to call robbing. Easy apartment blocks, difficult Hotels like, The German Hotel, just on the outskirts near the banana plantation that had a security guard.

It was a little embarrassing being a Hibs supporter at that time. Hibs are a club with a proud history but very little trophy success and had a terrible derby record at that particular time. Therefore, we weren't very optimistic about our chances of a result.

Being an Old-Firm fan, as Rangers and Celtic are known, is quite different. Both clubs are steeped in tradition and shared trophy success. They can look forward to the outcome of a match with equal amounts of optimism as both were capable of winning.

So, we didn't talk about football for very long.

I was more interested in learning as much information about Malia and who to be wary of and who was trust-worthy.

We went to a club called 'Krypton' that night. It was the best club for Dance music, which was just beginning to take off in Crete at that time. This was due to the influence of the American Dj's from the nearby Air Force base playing the most recent music, and one Dj in particular, called 'Cisco'.

When I was back home in Edinburgh very few people from the housing schemes were into Dance music. It was a much more esoteric scene in Edinburgh. People who were into fashion and musical trends.

A lot of the recently formed Hibs casuals, the CCS, or Capital City Service, as they were known, followed fashion, due to the nature of being a 'casual' and not wearing a football scarf. They frequented the small number of clubs catering to this type of music, which had only been around two years previously with the advent of the Acid-house movement, around '87. This deterred a lot of youths from schemes travelling into the nightclubs in town because of the violence associated with the casuals.

Anyway, we were all there dancing and drinking, when I started to notice all these men moving around us. I thought it was because we were the only guys dancing. There were about ten of them. Big well-built men with crew cuts. I assumed from the Air-Force base. I pointed them out to Andy who had also became aware of their presence. I nodded at Tim and Dom. They stopped dancing and came and stood beside us. The men stood still not making eye contact.

"Who the fuck are they?!" I asked.

Tim and Dom shrugged.

Then Dave piped up, "I had a bit of bother with them last night."

"Who are they?" Andy asked.

"A bunch of Geordies," Dave replied.

"How many's a bunch?!"

"There were about thirty or forty last night."

We all looked at each other, this lot were sent to get us outside.

"Our best bet is to set about this lot in here," I said, "Cos if they get us outside and there's another thirty, we're fucked!"

Nobody wanted to make a decision but somehow, we had edged towards the door.

The outside of Krypton had a large covered porch. Once outside we were now surrounded on this porch. Dave wasn't exaggerating about the numbers. There was easy forty of them. Big muscle-bound Geordie bastards. They looked like a football crew.

"I told you coming outside was a big mistake! Everybody stand together. No running. Just stick tight and don't run in."

My words were drowned out as the place erupted! They showered us with bottles and threw chairs at us. We tried to scramble for shelter but there wasn't any. We backed off into the street still in a huddle facing them as they encircled us. For some reason they didn't charge at us. Dom suddenly charged forward at them. He was immediately dropped.

Andy broke ranks to run and help Dom and I stepped forward instinctively to have Andy's back. He grabbed Dom and helped him to his feet, still the Geordies didn't charge us, we just all stood bouncing on our feet in anticipation. They began pelting us with bottles again. We had our arms up to protect our faces and tried throwing bottles back. I thought it would never end until a shout went up that they had hit a Greek with a bottle.

Silence. You could have heard a pin drop. We stood still. The Geordies stopped.

"They've cut a Greek!" Andy roared.

Honestly. I had never seen a fight change so quickly. Greeks appeared from everywhere and charged the Geordies, who froze. We didn't. We steamed in, throwing punches, Andy at the front.

Old Greek men from restaurants steamed in, young Greek men from clubs steamed in. Greeks of all ages attacked the Geordies.

Andy bellowed as he fought, "They cut a Greek!"

The Geordies panicked, turned, and started to run. We chased after them. Andy leading the charge, an army of Greeks at the back of us. Now I knew how Alexander had felt!

The Geordies threw a CS gas canister at us. Who takes that on holiday?! We ran through the smoke and jumped over the canister. We ran them up the Beach road. More Greeks came out to join us.

"They cut a Greek!" a voice shouted again.

The Greeks from the kebab shops were armed with machetes and meat cleavers.

The Geordies were scared now. Andy was screaming from the front, "CCS! Geordies on the run!"

We had now run the length of the Beach road and were still chasing them up into the old town. Yet more Greeks joined us asking what had happened.

"They cut a Greek with a bottle!" Andy informed them.

An older Greek stopped us at a doorway. He opened a cupboard door and started handing out brand new pick-axe shafts! I swear it was like a scene from an old Western when they start handing out the Winchesters to the posse!

Armed now with pick shafts we continued to bay for blood, to avenge our fallen Greek comrade.

Out of a doorway ahead of us, a guy appeared, on his own, and started walking towards us. Somebody grabbed him, and he started yelling he was from Liverpool. I swung my shaft at him, but he leant back, and I just missed connecting with his head. He took off like rocket.

"What are you doing, Kenny?!" Andy yelled.

"Why did he say he was from Liverpool? How did he know we were after Geordies!"

"Bastard!" Andy called, and we took off after him.

We caught sight of him just as he entered an apartment block.

Two girls standing outside said, "They're not in there."

I was ready to swing my pick again.

"How do you know who we're after, you stupid cows!" Andy caught them out.

They realised their mistake and the stupidity showed on their faces.

One Greek guy produced a canister containing petrol and started to pour it around the apartment block!

The owner came running out, arms in the air, shrieking in Greek. He pleaded to a couple of the older men. They told us to go and that they would take care of it.

That was that. It was over as quickly as it had begun.

We swaggered back down through the village, stopping to hand our pick shafts back in and I made a mental note where they were kept.

The next day, Sunday, we were having lunch in a place called 'Electra', at the bottom of the Beach road. They served a lunch of roast beef and Yorkshire puddings on a Sunday, so that was our Sunday ritual. The owner told us that the Geordies had been moved to another resort.

We had our noses in the papers, which were a day late, picking out team news from the previous day's Derby, when three girls walked in and stopped to say hello to Andy.

The one doing the talking was tallest, with brown hair and attractive. Another one, tall and less attractive, tartier, always pouting, but it was the smaller, prettiest of the three who I 'caught eyes' with, just for the briefest of moments.

Even though we had money, Tim wanted to do another 'mission' that night. We arranged to meet at 11.30 pm.

The four of us left Tim's apartment and headed to where the job was. As we neared a building, Tim slowed up and with his hand down by his side, imperceptible to anyone watching, slightly pointed his finger in its direction. Andy and Dom volunteered to keep watch.

We sneaked along through somebody's side garden to the back of an apartment block. The back wall of the property was level with the first-floor window of another apartment block. It was easily accessible. The only problem was that we were entering from someone's garden. So, the most important thing for me and Tim was that nobody came home once we were inside or we'd be caught, as that was our only escape route.

Andy and Dom had to be on the ball.

We were just about to climb through the window when a light came on.

We climbed back down the wall and decided to tell Andy and Dom that we would have to wait a while and didn't want them worrying about what was taking us so long, or thinking we'd been caught.

As we stepped out of the garden a Greek guy walked right past us. He didn't seem to notice us at first. Tim realised he had left his small tool-kit lying in the garden and made to go back for it. The guy came around the corner again.

Some look-outs Andy and Dom were!

I pretended I was drunk and leaned against the garden wall as if I was being sick. Tim held on to my arm to steady me. The guy approached us.

"I'll ram the head on him Tim, then we run like fuck!" I whispered.

"No don't!" Tim pleaded, then turned to the guy. "He's ok, he's just had too much to drink."

"Come with me!" The guy took my other arm in a vice-like grip, "I live just here."

We're caught I thought. But the guy turned out to be the kindest person you could meet! He took us into his house, sat me at his kitchen table and brought me a glass of water! I sipped at the water still thinking it was a trap. I told him I felt much better now. He wished us goodnight and we staggered outside back into the street. Once out of view Tim dropped his arm from my shoulders and the consequences of anyone finding his tool-kit hit him.

He told me he had stolen the tool-kit from his landlady and that they were already under suspicion. If the screwdrivers were found they'd be caught!

I tried to reassure Tim that we would get the bag back, but I was struck by the stupidity of using something you'd borrowed from your landlady to break into apartments. The one thing that could identify you and tie you to the crime.

We trudged down through the village and came upon our trusty look-outs.

"Where the fuck were you two?!"

Tim didn't give them time to explain themselves, he proceeded to tell them we nearly got caught. He relayed the story and I watched their faces in mock concern until he dropped the bombshell about the tool-kit and screwdrivers.

Dom's face changed, to panic. He knew it was them that were in trouble, not me and Andy. Andy's face changed, to relief.

"We can't go back for them. So, you two will have to," Tim stated.

The penny dropped, along with their bottle.

Andy started walking away saying he needed a drink first.

Dejectedly, we traipsed down, stopping at a Greek bar, 'Minolis'.

Andy ordered a round of beers and a shot of spirits for himself. Then Andy and Dom started playing cards! It was now obvious that they didn't want to go back for the bag.

Tim was looking very anxious. He was really worried about it.

"Are you two going or not?" I asked.

"In a minute," Andy answered, then ordered another round of beers.

"Fuck you's. C'mon Tim, lets go. I'll get them." I said.

Andy and Dom didn't even look up, and we left them playing cards as we made our way back up into the old-town.

"Do you see what I mean now, Tim, about not giving a share to people who don't do anything?"

Tim just looked at me. The reality of getting caught was really hitting home.

We got back to the gate, and I was just about to go into the garden when this Greek guy stepped out from behind a tree.

"Where are you going?" he said in broken English.

"We are lost," Tim tried.

I started walking away.

"Tim, c'mon walk. Quick, nash," I whispered, "Start walking."

Tim stopped to protest his innocence. The guy slapped him across the face.

"You bastard," he said flatly. Tim put his hands up to his face.

"No. No. I good boy," he protested.

"No. No. You bastard." The Greek guy slapped him again.

Tim was still trying to justify himself. I grabbed him by the arm, and half shoved the guy, who seemed drunk.

"C'mon Tim." I pulled at him.

"You thief. You bastard!" The guy shouted after us, but he didn't follow.

We quickened our step until we were out of sight, then legged it down to 'Minolis'.

Andy and Dom were still playing cards. We started to tell them what had happened but as were telling them, we saw the Greek guy and some others heading towards Tim and Dom's apartment. Tim and I took off and told Andy to meet us in the London pub.

Tim and I were sitting in the London pub drinking Jack Daniel's, trying to calm Tim's nerves. I was trying to console him, telling him that they didn't have any proof, but we both knew that over there they didn't need any.

Andy and Dom pulled up on the bike with bad news. They were searching Tim and Dom's apartment. They also said it would be impossible to get the tool bag back now.

Tim and I left the London pub and wandered aimlessly down the beach road. I had that horrible feeling in the pit of my stomach when you get caught. Andy and Dom rolled down beside us on the bike.

We stopped outside a café that was closed and sat on the steps. Tim sat with his head in his hands. He looked close to tears.

I knew the only real evidence they would have would be the tool bag.

I felt sorry for Tim. His cousin stood there silently, and his new mate Andy chewed his lip in mock concern, as if contemplating some solution.

"I'll go back up on the bike with Andy to see if I can get it, Tim." I said finally.

Tim perked up a bit and looked at us pleadingly.

"Aye. We'll go up and see if we can get it Timmy," Andy said, full of bravado. "Don't worry, mate."

We climbed on the bike and headed up to the old town. Andy took the long way around this time, so we came upon the house we were going to from the other side. It was just as well. The doorways of the neighbouring house had Greeks hanging around in them, trying to look inconspicuous, but only succeeding in the opposite.

We drove past without a second glance. Andy then slowed the bike to a halt and cut the engine.

"Fuck that, Kenny!" He said, "I'm not risking going in there for they tools now, and neither are you. It's me and you over here Kenny. Fuck them. Let Dom go back for them if he's that bothered about them getting caught."

I was disappointed in Andy. I felt that he had already let me down. He told me back home how pally they all were. How they all stuck together. How easy the robbing was and yet once we got here, he was reluctant to even keep watch. I knew that if it hadn't been for Tim, I would still have my twenty quid in my pocket.

Andy started the bike again.

"We can't do anything now anyway," he said and drove back down to the beach road.

Tim and Dom were still sitting on the café steps where we had left them.

"It's impossible, Tim," I told him. "There are Greeks everywhere, just waiting for us to go back."

Tim was frantic now.

"We have to get them back, Kenny. We're done for if they find them." Andy tried to reassure him and failed to catch my look.

We sat on the steps in complete silence. I suspected that I was the only one trying to think of a solution. Tim was too busy worrying about the consequences. Dom said nothing, and who could tell what Andy was thinking.

"What's at the back of that wall?" I asked out loud.

Tim looked up. Andy's face came to life at the same time.

"It's a piece of waste ground, Kenny," he said. "You can drive right up into the top of the village and get across it."

Andy was first on the bike and was some way to redeeming himself in my eyes.

We sped off up into the old town again, Andy negotiating the narrow alley-ways with ease. We drove on, then Andy stopped the bike and headed off, jogging. I followed him through an apartment block and then across a piece of waste-ground. We were running and stumbling over the uneven surface. We came to a fenced off garden.

"It's through there Kenny, and over that wall," Andy said, pointing.

I climbed the fence into someone's garden, edged along the side of their house until I was face to face with the wall.

I stepped back and ran at it, hauling myself up. Ironically, I was level now with the original apartment block that we were going to rob!

I dropped down as silently as I could. It was pitch black, so I felt my way along the edge of the garden path. I could see the lit cigarette ends of the Greeks in the doorways, waiting for us.

I searched blindly with my hands until I touched the small leather bag. I opened it to check that the screwdrivers were inside, and it hadn't been left as bait, then stuffed it into the waistband of my jogging bottoms and tied the string tight. The wall was smaller on this side, so I pulled myself up onto the ledge, pausing only to gaze mischievously at the apartment we were going to rob. Another time.

Once down on the other side, I made my way hastily back to Andy.

"Did you get it, mate?" he asked, anxiously.

"Aye," I nodded.

Andy's face lit up.

"Well done young gun! Let's bolt."

We ran back to the bike. Laughing and pushing each other as we stumbled over the waste-ground, relieved that the pressure was off.

Tim couldn't have been more grateful.

"Thanks Kenny. I owe you one." He shook my hand warmly. His tear-filled eyes conveyed all the thanks that was necessary.

Andy got the beers in and him and Dom cheered up considerably. I sat out on the pavement with Tim as he continued to thank me.

"There's no need to thank me Tim. You did me the favour by going crooking with me. I'd have been fucked if it wasn't for you."

"That's it for me now, Kenny. I'm going home. Me and Dom have been talking about it and when my dad leaves tomorrow, we are going with him. We've had enough."

My heart sank.

"Tim if you go home now, I'm fucked."

"I'm sorry Kenny, but that's it. We're off."

Even though I'd only known Tim for a couple of days, I'd taken to him. Perhaps it was because he seemed like-minded. Maybe it was just because he had the bottle to do what I thought we were all here to do. Anyway, whatever the reason, I was sorry he was going.

"Honestly, Kenny. I feel shit about leaving you in the lurch like this, but this was too close a shave. I feel shit about it but..."

The rest of the night was a pisser for me. We had a few drinks together and met Julian later on. Who, it was decided, would now move in with Andy and me.

Mon 28th Aug.

I was in bed when Andy woke me.

"Kenny. Tim and Dom are leaving soon, and Julian's found us a new apartment, so get your stuff packed."

I got up, showered and dressed.

We packed our things and headed down to the taxi rank. The heat was intense, I could feel it burning into the back of my neck, so on the way, we stopped the bike and I got off, stealing a hat from a shop to shade my neck and face.

We all gathered for a group photo. Lloyd, Andy, Dom, Tim, and me. Kneeling at the front, Julian and Dave. Tim's dad took the picture.

I was gutted inside but forced a smile.

I shook Tim's hand through the taxi window and he sort of shrugged at me apologetically.

The taxi drove off and we stood there for a few moments, each of us in quiet contemplation.

"C'mon then," Julian said, picking up his bag and his Jim Morrison album, An American Prayer.

We drove along beside him with the bags, for a few hundred yards and stopped outside an apartment block on the main road called, Pension Eva.

The landlady was a nice woman called Maria. She showed us to our room on the first floor. There was a double bed to our right as we walked in, Julian threw his bag down on it.

"Is that your bed then, Jules?" Andy said, dead-pan.

To our left was a dividing door and two single beds. I took the one on my left. It was 1000 drachs per day each. We gave her 2000 drachs each and she left.

We sank down onto beds and lay in silence. Each of us lost in our own personal reflections.

We went through to Hersonisos that night for a few drinks at the Star bar. Just me and Andy, but we had a good laugh. Julian worked there, at the main disco, Aria, and he told us to meet him there later on after he had finished work.

Aria was a big sophisticated club compared to Flash or Krypton, but it was still a bit tacky for us. Cod dance music for the European crowd and the song 'French Kiss' was the big tune at the time. They used to play it at least ten times per night. Anyway, it was about 3 am and Julian, Dave and I wanted to go home to Malia as we were all pretty drunk, but Andy wanted to stay and go back to the Star bar as it was open until 5 am.

None of us could be bothered, it was all a bit flat, now that Tim and Dom had left.

Andy got a bit ratty.

"Well go then," he snapped.

"Andy," I tried to reason with him, "you've got the bike, our bike."

"Look. I'm not going home just yet. I'm going to the Star bar."

Julian suggested us taking the 'big bike' as you could get three on it and Andy take Dave's scooter, which we nicknamed the Chicken Chaser.

"That'll be fuckin' right," Andy spluttered. "I can just see me pulling up outside the Star bar on that wee thing!"

Image was a big thing over in Crete. Image and bike size.

"Well, how the fuck am I supposed to get back, Andy?" I said.

We stood arguing for a time then me and Andy told each other to fuck off. Andy left to go to the Star bar. We stood outside while Dave got the Chicken Chaser started.

"I'll take Julian home and then come back for you," he offered.

Julian was looking around him at all the bikes parked up. He pulled a small penknife from his pocket and said, "Back in a bit."

I watched as he wandered around the parked bikes. He stopped at a 125. Checking the steering lock wasn't on, he turned his knife in the ignition and kick started the bike.

Pulling over to me, he told me to hop on.

"How the fuck did you do that?" I asked.

"The ignition locks are all worn with all the use they get, you can usually use any keys to start them. Or knife," he added, smiling. It was the first time I had seen him smile.

Then he sped away from Aria with me on the back, laughing.

Dave followed behind on his chicken chaser. We kept slowing down for Dave to catch us then pulling away again, so he didn't have to drive back on his own.

Andy didn't come back home the following day. I thought he was just still in the huff, so I didn't think much about it.

I sat at the pool all day on my own, listening to music.

Come night time, Andy was still in Hersonisos. When Julian was going to work at Aria that night, he told me that he would look out for Andy.

I went out myself that night and wandered down the beach road, stopping outside Flash to talk to Dave, for a second. He took me inside and had a beer with me at the bar, but it was empty and depressing.

I had a few beers, but felt a bit awkward drinking on my own, so I headed back up to the apartment about twelve o'clock.

It was really hot, and I couldn't sleep. I pulled a chair out onto the balcony and sat with my legs over the wall, listening to some music on a tape recorder.

I was listening to a song called The Paris Match. I'd brought a tape from home with me that had four Style Council songs on it, from an early concert in May '83, that were deeply personal to me. I used to listen to it endlessly throughout the summer of '83, especially at night, when I was alone, and struggling to come to terms with my mums illness.

It was about 2 am when, Julian, passing, saw my feet hanging over the ledge.

"Kenny," he called up softly. I popped my head over.

"I've got some bad news. Andy's been in a fight in Hersonisos and had his ear bitten off..."

My heart sank. "What happened?"

"I don't know. I only just got told by chance, off this girl."

I ran down the stairs, passed Julian, and ran down to Flash. I borrowed Dave's scooter from him. I told him that I wanted to go through to Hersonisos to find Ian and find out what had happened.

I drove through to Hersonisos in a daze. I couldn't believe that something like this could happen to someone like Andy.

I drove straight to the Star bar, only to be told that Ian had pissed off with a girl.

I was raging at this.

The guy on the door said that Ian would be back by 4.30 am.

I didn't fancy hanging around for two hours, so I drove back through to Malia. I went back to Flash and told Dave that I would need his bike to go back later when Ian went back to work.

I drove around on the bike for a while, dazed, trying to gather my thoughts. Everything seemed faintly ridiculous. Everybody drunk, and in good spirits, milling about the streets, oblivious.

I looked at them all, faces contorted into that stupid drunken gargoyle expression. I saw them for what they were, and I hated them. Pitied them. Indulging in this pathetic escapism, an Odyssey that lasted all of two weeks. The splendour of the ancient Greeks lost on them. The birthplace of democracy. The exploits of Alexander and Odysseus meaningless to them as they cavorted inanely. I kept thinking how my pal had just lost his ear.

I left the Beach road and drove up into the old town for some sanity. The comparisons were ludicrous, and I struggled to find a happy medium. I stopped the bike and got off. The sky was beautiful and clear, the moon full and brilliant and the stars sparkled knowingly.

I realised I was outside the church just off the main road. It was framed perfectly in this scene of stars and sky. It reminded me instantly of the postcards I'd seen over here 'From here, to Eternity.'

I shuddered involuntarily, like someone had walked over my grave. I jumped back on the bike and headed left onto the main road and out of Malia. The night sky was blue and shades of purple, no clouds only clarity. I raced on, head bent over the handle bars as I cleared Stalis. I was out on the open road when the night seemed to close in on me, the sea to my left became black and menacing. I wished I had a faster bike. I relaxed as I saw the welcoming lights of Hersonisos up ahead and slowed down as the town lights embraced me.

As I approached the door of the Star bar, Ian saw me. He looked fairly complacent.

"What the fuck happened to Andy?!"

"How are you doing mate?" he offered, pathetically, "Oh, he got his ear bitten off last night."

"By who?!"

"Some Greek Germans."

"What happened?!"

"Andy was with this bird and the guy said something..." Ian hesitated. "I didn't really see what happened..."

I cut in, "What did you do?!"

"I tried to jump in for him, but I was drunk and sort of fell as I tried to throw a punch..." his voice tailed off.

I stared at him blankly, wanting to make his explanation difficult. "Ian. When the fuck were you thinking of telling me all this?!" He looked at me meekly.

"It's been two fucking days!" I said. "I only found out through Julian, and he only found out by accident! So, when were you thinking about telling me?"

"I tried to borrow a motorbike to get through..." He was shaking.

"That's a fuckin' lame excuse. Why not get a taxi? Or a fuckin' bus?!"

"Honestly, Kenny. I was dead upset. I had to get a drink to calm down..."

I walked away leaving him feebly trying to justify his actions, or lack of them.

In retrospect I should have battered him. At the time though I was more concerned about Andy than angry with Ian. Even now I hope his lack of courage haunts him. But knowing how gutless he is, it probably won't.

Wed 30th Aug.

Early that morning me and Julian went to Alex's bike shop on the main road to hire a motorbike for the journey through to Heraklion Hospital to see Andy. Heraklion is the capital of Crete and about thirty to forty miles away.

Julian was telling Alex what happened to Andy. Alex offered to give us a red Vespa for the afternoon, for free. Thanks Alex.

Julian used to carry this brown leather wallet type purse thing with him all the time with a wrist strap and a zipper and a hidden compartment inside. I remember him zipping it closed when Alex said he didn't want any money.

We climbed on the Vespa and drove out of Malia on our way to Heraklion.

I wasn't very keen on motorbikes, due to a bad crash I'd had three years previously, and never felt safe on a bike with Andy, but Julian was a considerate driver and I didn't have to look over his shoulder at the road and circumnavigate. I could relax.

We hardly spoke as we drove, which suited me. I was worried what state Andy was in. We passed through the now familiar, Malia and Stalis on towards Hersonisos driving through little unknown towns. Small, perfect, idyllic.

I recall us driving through Kokiki Hani. There is a small flat stretch of beach, then the road arcs sharply to the right as you round the bend and an island comes into view. For some reason it reminded me of the island in 'Dr No'. Perhaps because I was on an adventure and drawing comparisons to other adventures. Who knows? I mentioned it to Julian all the same. He just lifted his head, smiled and said, "Yeh," and kept on driving.

Further on we drove, and every resort now seemed smaller than the last and the age of the inhabitants seemed to increase, they now looked less inviting, only more desperate.

The drive seemed to be taking an eternity. Extended periods on bikes with no music to punctuate your thoughts seem to last forever.

Finally, up ahead on the right, we saw Heraklion Airport.

On our left were the permanent Gypsy camps, like a deserted rubbish tip. Birds hovered overhead, swooping down to feed on scraps.

Their houses appeared to be made of impossibly fragile structures, resembling sheets of paper with squares cut out of them and assembled with shattered plywood, hopefully pieced together. They flapped in the breeze.

Sheets of polythene and shards of cardboard, bending futilely against an indiscriminate wind.

What at first looked like a rubbish tip on closer inspection were in fact the collapsed 'houses'.

Skinny old dogs and kids in rags wandered around this desperate landscape. It might have been dogs in rags and skinny old kids.

It felt such a pointless existence.

'JUST CLOSE YOUR EYES AGAIN UNTIL THESE THINGS GET BETTER'

Entering Heraklion, the traffic was chaotic. Cars, buses, and trucks honking horns and drivers shouting and gesturing aggressively. Pulling over to ask for directions, we were treated with ignorance and indifference. Obviously, the capital doesn't rely on tourism.

At last, somebody was sympathetic on hearing that we were trying to find the Hospital and gave us exact directions.

I remember driving down this lovely green leafy road, lined with pine trees, when we spotted this impressive looking building.

Julian noticed the Hospital sign and drew up in the carpark.

Julian put the bike on its stand and we started walking towards the main entrance. I started to get butterflies in my stomach. Once inside the building we stopped at the reception desk to ask directions to Andy's ward.

As we went along the corridors, we were shocked at what we saw. Two dead bodies lying on trolleys with white sheets pulled up over their heads but their cold dead feet sticking out the bottom, wrinkled and blue.

A cat in the corridor sniffing at a litter bin, jumped up onto one of the bodies. Nobody cared.

The corridors smelled terribly. Not with that horrible disinfectant smell you normally associate with hospitals, but just stale and dirty.

We had to enter Andy's ward through the washroom. The sinks were on the opposite side to the urinals and the toilet cubicles lined the left-hand wall. The place stank of urine. There was an open door on the right that led into the ward!

The noise was incredible. Patients groaning and visitors sobbing un-controllably. We heard the toilets flushing loudly.

We walked into the ward.

Andy's bed was the first one on our right. He was lying with his back to us, curled up in the foetal position. He looked puny and pathetic. His arms and legs were exposed, and I could see his skin was dirty and his usual healthy tan had an unusual pale sickly pallor to it and he lay motionless. His head was swathed in a huge discoloured bandage, with a large red patch over his left-hand side where his ear had been. He looked crumpled, dishevelled and unwashed. Flecks of dirt and grime and blood had transferred from his body onto the already disc-oloured bed sheets.

I turned and walked out before he could see me.

Julian came after me and caught my arm.

"C'mon, Kenny."

"For fuck sake, Julian. Look at him. I don't want to see him like that."

"Come on, you've got to."

We re-entered the ward.

"Andy," Julian said softly.

Andy turned around. His dulled eyes brightened up when they saw us. "Aah, how you doin' lads?"

"We're alright Andy," I said. "What about you?"

"I got my fuckin' ear bitten off Kenny."

"What happened?!"

"Ach, it was a stupid fight over a girl."

"What did Ian do?"

"He did nuthin'. Seriously. Fuck all. It was these German Greek guys outside the Star bar. They were standing around next to their bikes. I went over with her to get on mine and as she was climbing on this one guy said something. I said to him, 'What was that mate?', and he just grabbed me and bit my ear off. So, we started fighting. Some guys I knew from the bar broke it up and kicked the fuck out of the guy. They gave him a real beating, jumped on his arms to break them. Then somebody said that my ear was missing, and I just wandered around trying to find it." His voice was a hoarse whisper.

I felt terribly at the thought of my friend wandering around trying to find his missing ear.

"Fuck me," I heard Julian utter almost inaudibly.

Andy continued, "Then they put me in a taxi to take me to hospital, and I was just sitting there mate, holding my fuckin' ear in my hand!"

Andy suddenly stopped speaking and just stared straight ahead, trancelike.

Julian and me, looked around the ward awkwardly, unable to comment. Unable to find any words of solace.

There were three other beds in the room. One to Andy's right, and two directly opposite him. One was occupied by an old man, who looked like very shortly, he would be joining the queue in the main corridor. The other bed was partially obscured by a group of relatives, busy doing his fetching and carrying for him. The bed to Andy's right was covered by a screen.

"This place is a disgrace," I couldn't help but say.

Andy broke out of his reverie.

"Kenny, I've been here for two days and I haven't seen anybody yet. Not even a nurse. Look at these bandages. They must need changed?"

He was right. They were filthy.

"That's why these people have their relatives in," he continued. "See if the beds weren't taken, the relatives would be sleeping in them!"

We laughed at the absurdity of this. Probably nerves too. Even Andy laughed.

"Have you got any smokes, Julian?" Andy asked.

"Yeah." Julian reached into his pockets.

"We'll go out onto the balcony." Andy pointed, getting out of bed "I wouldn't want to get any more germs in here!"

We pushed open the glass doors and stepped onto the balcony. A young Greek girl was sitting there smoking and she looked up and smiled at us and said 'hello' to Andy.

"See if it wasn't for her, Kenny. I'd be fucked," Andy said as she went inside passing him.

"Why? Who is she?"

"She's been here visiting someone, but she brings me fags and things to eat. I've not been fed for two days! Honestly! I haven't seen a nurse! There was a cat on that old guys bed earlier!" he exclaimed. "A cat!"

"It's in the corridor now!" I said, flatly.

"This is a fuckin' joke!" Andy blurted out. "A fuckin' joke!" He repeated.

I kept looking at his face. As I've said, Andy was a good-looking lad and to see him like this was ridiculous. I couldn't believe how calm he was.

The balcony had benches and we sat on them looking out across the landscaped grounds.

Andy and Julian drew deeply on their cigarettes.

"We need to get you out of here as quickly as possible, mate."

"Kenny, see when they first brought me in? They stitched my ear back on without an anaesthetic. It was pure agony. I could feel every stitch going in. Honestly mate. See now? I just want to go home."

"What are we going to do about that? We don't have any money."

"Ian's going to go and see the British Consulate. I'll be in here for a few days yet. How did you get through here by the way?"

"Julian got a bike from Alex."

"Cheers, Jules."

"He only gave it to me for a few hours, so we'd better get going."

"When will you come again?" Andy asked, pitifully.

"We'll try and come tomorrow, if we can get a bike sorted out."

"I've got some money." Julian offered.

"Is there anything you need, Andy?" I asked.

"An ear." He stared off into the distance again. "Something to eat, mate. Some fags. Cheers."

"Pizza crisps and Milko, Andy?!"

He laughed. "Aye, cheers, Kenny. Thanks for coming lads, see you later."

We were embarrassed.

"See you tomorrow, Andy," we chorused as we left him behind.

Me and Julian were silent as we made our way back out along the corridor out of the hospital and back to the car-park. It was hard to take things seriously in this heat. It seemed to trivialise everything. Back home bad news was so easy to equate with bad weather. This was different. To feel bad when you felt good.

We walked over to the Vespa. Julian got on started it and then rocked it forward off its stand.

"This place is a dump," I stated.

"He doesn't look too bad though," said Julian, trying to sound positive.

"Aye, he seems to be taking it well."

"Come on. We have to get this bike back and I have to get ready for work."

"Right. Thanks Julian."

It just struck me. I didn't even know Julian. I hadn't even spoken to him before. We drove back in silence.

We took the bike back to Alex. Julian asked how much to hire it for the week. Alex said 10,000 drachs, which was a good price.

Julian opened his leather wallet and paid him.

While we were driving along to Pension Eva, I told Julian that I didn't have any money. I also confided in him that now Tim was gone, and Andy was in that state, I was fucked.

I lay on my bed in the apartment while Julian got himself ready for work.

"I'll try and get you a job beside me," he said.

"Doing what?"

"At Aria. You know, just past the Star bar where the road hits the pier and bends to the harbour? I work just there. Handing out leaflets to advertise Aria. It's dead easy and the pay is 4000 drachs per night."

"Julian, no disrespect, but I didn't come over here to do that."

"Oh yeh, I know. But it'll do for now. It's best to have a job, not just to fall back on, like now, but for cover as well. Tim an that were fuckin' stupid. No wonder they nearly got caught. He kept doing the same apartments every two weeks. He thought that just cos it were different people in them he was alright. He forgets it's the same owners!"

"So, you're up for it then?" I asked.

"Yeh. Too right. I'm just not fuckin' thick! What are you going to do tonight? D'you want some money to go down Beach road? Tell you what, why don't you come through to Hersonisos and I'll get you into Aria?

"Nah, I might just leave it tonight."

"Are you sure? What else are you going to do?"

"I might just have a wander 'round and see if I can find something for us. I need some time to think."

"Right then. I'm off. See you in a bit. I'll tell you what, I'll come straight back through after I've finished work and we'll go down the Beach road for a drink."

"Aye, ok." "Right, see ya."

The second the door closed behind him I felt alone. I kept going over the day's events in my head. I kept seeing Andy curled up on that hospital bed, his head swathed in filthy bandages, bloodstained.

I heard Julian start up the Vespa and instantly wished I had gone with him.

I decided to take a shower and wash the hospital off me. I put on all black, jogging bottoms and T-shirt. I slid open our balcony door and stepped outside.

Directly opposite our block was a gap between the houses that overlooked a basketball court. Beyond that was a clear patch of sky, light blue, purple, and a darker blue as the day turned into night.

Foreign skies that made me feel a longing for something. That indescribable yearning for something more. These romantic notions were ridiculous in comparison to my more immediate problems. Andy and money.

My reverie was interrupted by the sounds of girls giggling and the clicking of their heels on the pavement. What a sound! I turned my head to the left and caught sight of three girls, arms linked, tottering towards the Beach road. Tight tops, short skirts, high heels. The perfect combination. My spirits rose.

One of the girls must have saw me overlooking the balcony as she whispered something to her mates and they all looked up and laughed sexily.

I smiled down at them and watched their ample arses jiggling against the tight confines of their mini-skirts. You'll all be horizontal before the nights over.

I stepped back inside and locked the balcony door. You can't be too careful, I thought.

It was now almost completely dark as I wandered around the old town, gradually becoming familiar with each alley-way and where it led to.

Young people spilled from every building. All dressed in their best clothes, and of course, your arseholes in their various club football tops. I couldn't believe how many groups of people left the keys to the apartments in plant-pots right outside the doors! Just asking to be robbed, I justified it to myself. More and more people continued to pass me as I continued to meander. Too many for my liking. It was best not to get seen too often.

I made my way back down towards the main road, walking along and through the village to come down at the post office. I went back to our apartment and sat outside on the balcony and got lost listening to music.

I was in my own little world and came out of it by hearing Julian shouting up at me.

I must have had a bemused look on my face as I looked down at him over the balcony.

"What the fuck are you doing?!" he asked, half laughing.

"I must have drifted off..."

"Drifted off?!" he laughed now. "This is Malia Kenny, you don't drift off here mate, not with all this fanny about. C'mon!"

He seemed in good spirits.

I trotted down the stairs and approached the bike. "C'mon yi slow bastid. Get on!"

"What's the big rush?!" I asked.

"It was Tuesday last night, yeh?"

"Aye."

"Well? With all the fuckin' about with Andy and all that, I forgot all about it. It's when all the new arrivals get here, Tuesday!" He rubbed his hands gleefully. It was the first time I'd noticed his crooked smile. The best since Brando.

"So, some bird's getting it tonight!" he said making a fist.

We both laughed.

I'd never seen Julian display a sense of humour before. On first meeting him, it was more or less an arrogant 'alright' or 'see ya', or 'no ta'. I suppose he was maybe a little guarded at first, like I tended to be and now that it was only me and him, he had decided to open up a bit.

I climbed on the back of the bike and had barely got my balance before he pulled quickly away.

"Where did you go earlier tonight?" he asked, looking over his shoulder, as he darted between two cars and shot down the side road next to Galaxy bar.

"I just had a wander around the old town, looking at apartments." I said, raising my voice over the sound of the Vespa.

"All in black?! Kenny the Cat!" He laughed.

I smiled as I looked down at my all black apparel.

"You'll get us fuckin' nicked for prowlin' before anything else, Kenny!"

We both laughed this time. Julian hit a bump and I tensed, but he carried on unperturbed, accelerating out of it. He could sure handle a bike.

"Isn't this a one-way street?" I pointed out. "Yeah." He nodded coolly and left it at that.

He pulled the bike over outside 'Zig Zag'. Loud dance music reverberated against its full- length glass windows. It was much busier than usual, due to the new arrivals.

"I know a girl in here, we'll get free drinks." He was off the bike, had it on its' stand, and was swaggering in, all in one swift movement.

He carried himself well and had a very confident manner about him. His coolness was accentuated even more by his shoulder length hair, now I realised why Andy was so insistent on me getting mine cut! Tim and Dom also had longish hair and mines would have been about the same length as Julian's now. Long and blond! Nice one Andy!

I followed in behind as he approached a mini-bar on the right-hand side, just inside the front door.

A tall girl, with long brown hair, and a pleasant face greeted him with a warm smile.

"Hiya Julian." She said beaming, too obviously pleased to see him. "A'right Sharon". Julian smiled from the corner of his mouth. Brando again. She melted, visibly.

"This is Kenny, Andy's mate."

"Hiya, Kenny. Are you from Scotland too?" she asked cheerily.

I nodded trying to place her accent.

"Aye."

"How is Andy?"

"Never mind the pleasantries, Sharon," Julian cut in, "give us a drink first."

"Brandy, Julian? Is three-star all right?"

Julian tutted and rolled his eyes mockingly, "I suppose."

"Metaxa all right with you, Kenny?" she asked.

"Nah, I'll just have a coke please."

"You won't!" Julian broke in, deliberately broadening his Manchester accent. "Not if you're drinking with me, pal. You'll have a pint!" He winked at Sharon. "Give 'im a pint Sharon!"

Sharon looked at me, a little unsure, not wanting to upset Julian but not wanting to upset me either.

Julian's voice lightened, "Have a drink, Kenny. I hate drinkin' on me own."

Sharon looked at me.

"I'll have a bottle of beer, please," I said.

"Besides," Julian added quickly, "It's free."

I watched as Sharon poured Julian a huge measure of brandy and coke. She pulled the top off an Amstel for me.

"So, how is Andy now?!" she asked.

"He's not too bad," I replied.

"How did it happen?"

"I dunno, really..."

"Over a bird," Julian cut in, mimicking cynicism, shaking his head and tutting.

"Really?" Sharon went on.

"Aye as far as I know," I offered.

"What a shame," she sympathised.

Julian pushed his empty glass towards Sharon's arm, which she was resting on the bar.

"Oh? Do you want another one, Julian?!" Sharon had a warm, inviting demeanour and was clearly enamoured with Julian.

Looking at him now, as he smiled at her, and studying him for the first time. Even though he had the killer smile of Brando, he actually looked like Jim Morrison.

"Are you going to Krypton later?" she asked hopefully.

"Yeah," he answered. "Are you?"

"It depends on what time this place closes. If we miss Krypton, we'll probably go to The Kalia bar."

Julian drained his glass again, and she refilled it for him without prompting.

"Yeh. Are you up for that, Kenny?"

"What's that?" I asked, distracted, wishing I was somewhere else.

"The Kalia bar? It's an all-night bar just outside town. Mostly Greeks and workers, no tourists." Sharon informed me.

"Aye, ok."

We stayed and had a few more drinks, Julian and Sharon playfully flirting, and me casually watching the interplay.

The music was getting louder and faster and the bar was filling up with scantily clad holiday makers. I watched all the girls eyeing up the men, trying to catch the attention of the most handsome.

Julian turned around on his stool to face the open bar area as Sharon was busy serving. He cast his eye admiringly over the female clientele and smiled at me as he played the game with them.

"Oh, by the way. I've got you a job," he announced.

"Where?!" I was surprised.

"Beside me, like I said, in Hersonisos. Don't worry. Its dead easy. We stand out on the promenade handing out leaflets from 7.30 pm to 12.30 am, and it's 4000 drachs per night. Then, up to Aria for some free drinks. Either stay there or come home. The fanny is much classier through there, more Dutch and German and Scandinavian women, real lookers and filthy too. It's mostly English birds in Malia."

"4000..."

"That's good money, Kenny. Most people are only on 3000. The works dead easy, or I wouldn't be doing it either. It's only handing out leaflets."

"Aye, I know..."

"It'll do in the meantime. Just to let things calm down a bit."

I left it at that. Julian was right. It was a good idea to let things settle down.

"We'll just take it easy for a bit. Relax." He smirked. "Get you a bird."

He drained his glass, "You don't drink much for a Scotsman. Let's go to Krypton."

Krypton at this time was the best dance club on the Beach road. It was the only one that played decent dance music not just chart stuff. Most of the other bars were sort of holiday bars, playing summer records, you know. Agadoo or Opus 'life is life' profound stuff like that. Shit, in other words.

I'd been in Krypton before but this time it was even better.

Like I've said, the reason for the music being so good was the American Dj's from the Air-Force base. They had the most recent records.

Nearly all the other clubs insisted on having Greeks Dj's, who all insisted in swaying to the side in the Dj booths, stepping to and fro behind the decks, and shouting 'oh yeh' or 'come on' over their mikes, clicking their fingers out of time to the music. They all wore high-waist, tight stonewashed jeans, with braces, showing a little bit too much white sock above patent leather slip-on shoes. A bit Michael Jackson circa Thriller. But it was '89! So that gives you an idea about their taste in music.

England had had Acid-house for two years and groups like the Happy Mondays and Stone Roses were heading a new wave of bands. It was the first decent musical movement since punk.

Julian manoeuvred his way through the crowd to the bar and ordered two beers.

I suddenly remembered I didn't have any money. "Julian, I haven't got any money."

He chose to ignore me then passed me a bottle of beer and said, "Here, there you are."

We sipped at our bottles as we jostled through the crowds, drawing looks from the women before standing at the edge of the dance-floor.

"You get a lot of looks from women, Kenny, eh?" Julian remarked. It was true. I've never known why.

Julian stood on the edge of the floor, gently swaying and moving his hips. Then he put his bottle down and moved out onto the sparsely populated dance-floor. Wow. He was a brilliant dancer. Not overly theatrical, dipping and spinning around the floor, just a real sense of moving in rhythm. I wasn't getting many looks now. All eyes were on him. Even the men. Eyeing him enviously.

We spoke, but mostly drank, and chatted loosely to girls until the club was closing. It was the type of night when there were so many options you couldn't settle on one. We began making our way outside. Neither of us had been in a particularly good mood all night, probably due to the last few days with Andy and knowing we had committed to go and see him again the following day. Also, Julian had lost his earlier enthusiasm, and the fact I hadn't any money added to it all.

So, when we got outside, and Julian asked if I wanted to go to the Kalia bar, I said 'I couldn't be bothered.'

"Me neither." Julian agreed.

"What about that bird Sharon?"

Julian just smiled as he started up the bike, "She'll keep."

Thurs 31st Aug.

We got up early and showered and dressed in shorts and T-shirts as the heat was stifling. We searched out a pair of sunglasses, from our growing collection and both settled on green-tinted Aviators.

It's funny, my eyes are sensitive to bright light, but I didn't like wearing sunglasses in Crete, feeling that they dulled my vision and I wanted to see everything as it really was.

However, for practical reasons like now, I had to.

Julian unzipped his leather wallet, took some money out, and stuffed in into his denim cut-offs, "Are you right?"

I nodded. Then off we went again to visit Andy. We stopped once in Heraklion to buy Andy his rolls, crisps and chocolate Milko.

Andy was delighted to see us. He still seemed a bit dazed, but he ate his rolls, crisps and drank his Milko. I smiled at the deliberate way he ate. He wiped his lips.

"That was delicious!"

Julian handed Andy a cigarette from his own packet then handed him another two packets, whilst heading out onto the balcony.

"Cheers Jules!"

"Heard anything from Ian, Andy?" I asked.

Andy looked at me, as if carefully choosing his words, then, "He's a prick, Kenny," he said this with real venom.

That was it. He drew on his cigarette thoughtfully.

"I haven't even seen a nurse. Never mind Ian!"

We laughed hysterically at Andy's deadpan humour.

"Honestly," he continued. "If it wasn't for that lassie giving me food parcels, I would have starved." He laughed here to himself. "She's thinking of changing my bandages herself!"

We burst out laughing again.

Andy brought us back down to earth.

Staring out across the distance of the hospital grounds he narrowed his eyes and announced, "I've had enough. I just want to go home."

We shifted awkwardly in our seats. There was a long uncomfortable silence.

"We'll have to go soon Andy," I started to tell him. "I start a job tonight."

"What?!" Andy exclaimed. "Am I in a coma?! Julian, am I dreaming? I know I've only got one ear, but did I just hear him say he was starting a job? Kenny, I'm not well mate, this could be too much for me to take!" He clutched at his heart.

Andy tried his best to grin and wish me all the best but when I told him I was going to be working with Julian I saw his face drop slightly.

He looked as if he knew that his time here was over, and for us, it was only beginning. He knew what he would be missing, and I could see it in his eyes.

"A job will keep you going with money as well," he said, trying his best to sound upbeat.

Julian got up to leave.

"We'll see you again tomorrow, Andy."

Andy stayed out on the balcony, drawing deeply on his cigarette and looking reflective. I glanced back at him as I was leaving. His face was partially obscured by the huge bandage wrapped around his head. His left hand was up at the side of his head and his fingers were gently circling the outline of his ear.

'WE LIVE AS WE DREAM – ALONE'

After the long drive we got back to the apartment and dropped down on our beds. Julian flicked on the cassette player and I drifted off to the sounds of Van Morrison's new album, Avalon Sunset.

I awoke with Julian shaking my arm.

"Kenny!" he was saying, "C'mon, get up!"

"What time is it?" I muttered.

"Half-six. C'mon get up." He repeated.

As if to verify the time, the church clock just off the main street, chimed its half past the hour bells.

This was how we normally woke in the mornings, by hearing the chimes and listening intently to count how many. If you leaned right out over the balcony you could just make out the clock face but lying in bed and listening for the chimes was much easier.

"The water will still be warm for a shower," Julian stated.

The water was heated by solar panels during the day, so the water temperature only lasted until very early evening.

"Be quick though." He continued talking to me as I got up. "We can't be late. We have to go up to Aria first to collect the leaflets."

The first time I'd been to Aria was with Andy. The night he lost his ear.

Even though I didn't like the music, the club itself was impressive. It was a huge white building, with an inner hall encompassing a water fountain feature, that let the water run along the terrace outside. Only the music policy spoiled it. Cheesy European dance music and they played the song French Kiss at least a dozen times per night. The women were all much better looking than their Malia counterparts. Much more sophisticated but lacked the dress sense to compliment their looks. Still sporting big bouffant hairstyles and padded shoulders.

We picked up the flyers from the front desk and Julian introduced me to several members of staff, who acknowledged me with varying levels of indifference. It really was a lot snootier than Malia.

We went back outside and drove the short distance to the promenade. As we passed an apartment block, I recognised, I pointed up at a particular balcony.

"I've shagged a bird over that."

Julian looked up and grinned. We drove past the Star bar.

"I wonder if that prick Ian's been to the British Consulate yet?" I remarked.

"We'll go and see him later if you like," Julian said, twisting the bike to weave through the tourists. He spun the bike sharply to the left, shot along past a parked car, then pulled in abruptly.

"Here we are," he said brightly.

We dismounted and he put the bike on its stand.

The road ended here, but a narrow walkway existed that you could also drive a bike along.

We stood next to a wooden bench and a large wastepaper bin.

"Don't just hand the leaflets out to anyone. Make it young people and couples."

"Okay."

Julian approached tourists, offering them a flyer and a line in chat.

"Aria disco, free entry and one free drink with this flyer." He smiled charmingly.

Girls came in for special attention, and most of them, stopped and eagerly accepted the leaflets, the once over and the innuendo.

Lads got the leaflets, the barest information 'open late, free entry, one free drink' and a brash, 'cheers lads'.

The night passed fairly quickly, I must admit.

"Honestly Kenny, this must be the easiest job in Crete. No hassles, nobody watching over you. We could throw the flyers away and no one would know."

"Why don't we then?"

"Cos one guy did it and got battered, so it's best not to. Anyway, we'd still have to stand here 'til half-twelve, so what difference does it make? Come on. We'll go up to Aria for a quick drink then shoot home to Malia."

As it turned out, we stayed on in Aria till closing time, raising a glass for Van Morrison's birthday.

We were steaming drunk on the bike on the way home.

I told Julian it reminded me of a time Andy told me about when he was on the bike alone and driving between Malia and Hersonisos, late at night with the wind blowing against him and gunning the bike full throttle he used to sing the Queen song, 'Don't Stop me Now.'

'Don't stop me now. I'm having such a good time, I'm having a ball!'

'Don't stop me now, if you wanna have a good time just gimme a call!'

And, as he didn't know all the words in order, he would just sing out the words he knew and mumble the lines he didn't know, O'Gourly or O'Grady style, O'mumble sent the specials in....

'I'm a shooting star leaping through the sky, like a tiger defying the laws of gravity...'

'I'm a racing car passing by like mumble mumble...'

Then he would shout out the bit he did know

'I'm gonna go, go, go there's no stopping me!'

'I'm a sex machine ready to reload... I'm a mumble bomb about to explode...'

Then his favourite bit, at the top of his voice.

'I'm burning through the sky, two hundred degrees that's why they call me Mr Fahrenheit, I'm travelling at the speed of light! So, don't stop me. I don't want to stop at all...'

Julian laughed and said it was the only thing missing when riding a bike, music.

Fri 1st Sept.

We drove through to see Andy again. He seemed slightly better each day. He told us that Ian still hadn't been to see the British Consulate.

I don't know how Andy knew this, as all the time he was in Hospital, Ian never visited him. Andy said that Ian didn't have time, apparently.

I told Andy I would go and see Ian and find out why he hadn't been to see him.

On the way back home, we stopped off in Hersonisos and went to the Star bar. The guy setting up the bar told us Ian was around the corner at the New York bar.

We parked the bike and walked down to the shore front.

There was Ian. Sitting at a table with two girls eating a huge bowl of ice- cream with cherries and a sparkler and an umbrella. He was wearing sunglasses and a smirk. When he saw me approaching scowling, his face reddened. He started to stutter.

"Oh, eh... hiya Kenny. I've been meaning to come through and see you..."

I cut him short. "Have you been to the British Consulate yet?"

"I've been meaning to go....but it's hard. I was up all last night.. I couldn't sleep... I've not been able to drink, I've been so upset..."

"So, you haven't been?"

"Honest, Kenny. I've not had time..."

He must have saw my gaze switch from him to the ice-cream to the two girls as his voice tailed off again.

"But you've got time for ice-cream and tarts?! Ian, are you trying to take me for a prick?!"

"No, Kenny!" He sounded pathetic now. "I'm just as upset about Andy as you are, mate."

"I'm not your mate. If you're just as upset as me then how come you haven't even visited him in hospital?"

This should have been enough to even win over the girl's support, but for the menacing way I was leaning over him and spitting out my words, plus I'd called them tarts.

"Honest, Kenny, please sit down, mate. Have a drink." He looked around as if trying to get a waiter's attention or desperately looking for someone to save him.

"Fuck off, prick!"

I turned and walked out, and I haven't seen Ian McPake since.

Once we got outside Julian turned to me and said, "I thought you were going to twat him then!" Then he started laughing. "He fuckin' shit 'imself. I thought he were going to start cryin', me." He stopped laughing. "I would have battered him if I was you."

"It would have been a liberty, Jules. Ian's a sap."

"Oh, do you know Ian from back home then?"

I nodded.

"Can't he fight? Can you take 'im?"

"He's an arse."

"So, you can take him then?"

I forgot sometimes that Julian was only twenty years old. He appeared and acted a lot older. I suppose it was of importance amongst a group of young men like us. Me, twenty-three, Andy twenty-two, Tim twenty, Dom twenty, other Tim, Lloyd; like they had been doing at the pool, posturing, acting out, who could handle themselves, who couldn't. It didn't matter to me cos I always knew. So, when we stopped at the bike I just said, "Aye."

That night, the Friday, with Andy still playing on my mind, I wasn't really in the mood for getting drunk and pulling women. I didn't want to be a wet blanket either and tried to find a balance. I much prefer being alone when I have something I need to think through.

Julian must have sensed this and never pressed me.

He was alright that way Julian. He could also be quiet and introspective, but he could also let himself go and have a laugh. I was starting to think he was a good lad.

Like I said, I hardly knew him at all. Circumstances had dictated us having to spend time together and not once had he broached the subject of money. So far, he'd put his hand in his pocket and paid for everything, even for cold drinks during the day. The apartment, the bike, fuel, food for us and Andy. I suppose buying for two is like buying for one, but three? Those rolls, crisps and choco Milko all added up.

I'd never experienced this type of unselfishness before. Obviously, the odd mate had paid for a few drinks before on a night out, for example, but nothing like this.

I'd become totally dependent on this virtual stranger and unknowingly, so had Andy.

I remember us having a good laugh that night. We really seemed to hit it off. It helped that I wasn't so self-conscious handing out the flyers now and had started to join in the banter.

Later that night, when we had finished and had gone up to Aria, the owner told us we were being sent to work in 'Flash' in Malia. He was finding it difficult to get busy, so we were going to be the new 'Kamaki's. That's the name for standing outside and trying to attract people in. He was also cutting our wages from 4000 to 3000. Oh right!

Still I saw a bright side. "They must have sacked Dave!"

Julian looked pissed off.

"What's wrong?" I asked.

"Flash is fuckin' shit! It used to be really busy when I first came here, but now it's shit. It used to be like Krypton. Not now."

"How come?"

"I dunno. Sometimes the 'in' place just changes. Music policy? It doesn't help that its next door to 'George's' and 'Highway'. All the knob'eads from there start going and all the right people just fuck off. It's tacky as fuck as well, like a proper disco as opposed to a club, mirrored walls and coloured dance-floor and all that shit." He laughed.

If that wasn't bad enough, we now had to hand out flyers during the day on the beach.

"That's our days fucked now too! No more long lies!"

I wasn't too disappointed as I didn't know what to expect, but it put a real dampener on Julian.

"Come on we'll nip through to Malia and I'll show you Flash."

We got through to Malia and Flash was closed. It looked tacky even from the outside, really tacky.

The bars next door Julian had mentioned, Georges and Highway were just winding down and stragglers were heading down the beach road to Cosmos and Krypton, the two clubs that were open late.

When we got to Krypton, Dave was standing outside. Julian skidded the bike to a stop just missing his foot. He jumped back

"Fuck sake Julian, you shit me up then!" he said in his high-pitched voice.

"I hear you got the sack from Flash?"

"Yeah."

"Do you want to earn some extra money then?"

"Yeah."

Julian grinned. "Do us a favour tomorrow then."

"What is it?" Dave asked dopily.

"Pick up some flyers from Flash tomorrow morning and hand them out on the beach." He laughed.

"Why? Are you two working Flash now?! You bastards have got my job!" Dave moaned.

Julian tutted and raised his eyebrows.

"Yeah." He said flatly.

"Why can't you do it?" Dave asked.

"Cos we've got to visit Andy in 'ospital, that's why Dave."

"Oh yeah, how is he?"

Julian looked at me, "He's alright, Kenny, eh?"

"Aye, better than expected."

"How much will you give me?" Dave asked.

"How about a pound of flesh?" I cut in sharply, "Andy's ear do you?" I went on.

Dave laughed, half nerves, half guilt.

"I don't mean it like that, Kenny. I'm just asking."

Julian let him off the hook, "A 1000 do you?"

"A 1000!" I exclaimed.

"Yeah, that's fine that," said Dave, eagerly accepting.

"Right cheers then Dave." Julian put the bike on its stand and we headed up the stairs into Krypton.

"A 1000...." I started to say again.

"It's only 500 each, Kenny. It's a nightmare doing the beach. All you get is hassle. I'm telling you, its money well spent." And he nodded to himself in affirmation.

Krypton was busy, but Julian pushed his way to the bar and came back with two cold beers. We sipped at them and eyed up the talent. Julian nodded his head and swayed his hips in time to the music.

"C'mon." he said, tapping me with his elbow. "We'll head up to the dance floor and get a couple of drunken stragglers."

As we made our way through the throng of people a few girls' heads turned. He smiled knowingly as he knew their eyes were on him.

As the beers went down, we danced and swayed to the music. A couple of girls over by the Dj booth looked over and occasionally made eye contact, we danced towards them and beckoned them over at the same time. They neared us hesitantly.

I noticed Julian's dancing livening up a bit as the BPM of the music picked up. He moved his hips more like a woman than a man's when he danced, but not effeminate at all. Suddenly the music mixed into a really bassy tune, 'Humanoid', 'Stakker Humanoid' and Julian was away.

"This is me favourite this!"

He launched himself into the most amazing dancing I'd ever seen. He looked super cool. It's the only way to describe him.

Not like the twat dancers who try to show off at the local disco who are obviously into Northern Soul, dipping and spinning and twirling around to non-Northern Soul music.

This was just smooth, feet shuffling, arms gently swinging, sliding over and bending his knees then back up erect again, swaying with a brilliant look on his face.

The girls were both impressed, they couldn't fail to be, and I felt like a tit beside him. In fact, everyone on the dance floor near us was watching him. That's me fucked, I thought, as both girls watched him keenly.

As the bass faded into another tune, he just stopped where he was. Which was right next to the two girls. He drew a strand of hair slowly from his face, fixed his smile on them, leaned in close and said over the music.

"Are you coming over for a drink?"

They were already walking over towards me before he finished talking. I scanned their two faces looking for a reaction. One came. Well done Jules.

"This is Kenny," he said introducing me, as Julian had also been looking at their faces and he spotted the one who liked me.

"And I'm Julian." He fixed his eyes on his girl and smiled his brilliant smile.

We had a few more drinks with them. They were giggling provocatively and becoming more tactile with us.

Time to leave.

"Are we ready for the off then?" Julian asked, looking at me.

The girls giggled again. Ah, sweet music.

"Come on then." I went to put my arm around my girl and lead her out but suddenly and clumsily she grabbed me and started kissing me, moving her lips very fast and opening and closing them on mine, sticking her tongue deep into my mouth. My hand moved automatically for her breasts.

As if following her friends lead, the other girl attacked Julian with the same zeal. Julian's hand went straight between her legs. The girl tensed slightly, then melted deeper into him.

The sweet taste of alcohol on a girl's lips.

"Come on." We stopped kissing them simultaneously.

"Let's go."

Krypton was empty now as the lights came up and we all staggered outside.

"Our apartment's up in the old town," Julian's girl spoke.

"It's all right, we've got a bike." Julian nodded to the Vespa. "I'll take you up on it first, then come back for Kenny and your mate."

Julian kicked started the bike and rolled it off the stand. "Climb on."

A faint smile crossed his lips as she climbed on and her short skirt rode up to reveal her panties.

"Back in a bit, Kenny."

"We'll start walking up to the top of the road."

"Right." He nodded and pulled away, even managing to look cool on a Vespa, with his girl wrapping her arms around his waist and pressing the side of her face against his back.

We started walking, swaying, up the road. Me rubbing her arse and breasts and stopping for heavy petting sessions periodically on the way.

Julian was back for us just as we were reaching Flash. I let the girl get on first, then I swung myself over, pushing myself hard into her bottom, and her up against him. She put her hands around his waist, deliberately close to his crotch and I put my hands around her, tight against her breasts and his back.

Julian looked down into his lap at her hands and winked at me. "Hold on tight!"

Just then we both looked at each other realising that we were outside Flash. As if sensing that this was the beginning of our time.

I don't know how Julian kept the Vespa on the road. What with the speed he was doing.

He shot out of the opening at the top of the Beach road and up into the old town accommodating all the twists and turns of the narrow streets with ease. If it wasn't for the fact we had a girl on the bike with us I would have told him to slow down, but I didn't want to appear like a sap, especially as the girl seemed to be enjoying the thrill.

He skidded the bike to a halt and I eased myself off.

The girl, climbing off the bike after me, said, "He's mad on a bike him!" and staggered over to her pal.

Julian put the scooter on its stand and we made our way over to the girls. They were standing, leaning against each other, outside an apartment block.

"Which room's yours?" he asked.

They just looked at us and said, "We've lost our key."

"You're joking?!" I said. "Can't you just ask the owner to let you in?"

"Probably. But he wouldn't let us take you in..."

Julian cut this conversation short by taking his girl by the hand and leading her around the side of the apartment block to a building site.

I followed his lead and went to do the same.

"Where are we going?" My girl giggled as we stumbled through the darkness.

"Just here." I said, slipping my hand into her.

I could hear Julian and the other girl. So, presumably they could hear us, so, we both knew when we were finished.

"Are you ready, Kenny?" Julian sort of shout-whispered.

"Aye."

"Will I see you tomorrow?" the girl asked, the picture of innocence.

"Aye."

"Krypton?"

"Aye." I kissed her goodbye.

"See you tomorrow." She offered.

Julian and me emerged from the shadows together and headed for the bike. We both turned back and saw the girls meet together at the apartment, fixing their skirts and flattening their hair, whilst talking to each other.

Man, the drive back to Pension Eva was never sweeter.

'AND I WILL STROLL THE MERRY WAY AND JUMP THE HEDGES FIRST'

Sat 2nd Sept.

We went to see Andy again that morning. He was slightly better, but still all he wanted was to get home.

We sat out on the balcony as usual and Andy and Julian smoked. Andy sounded down.

"Honestly, Kenny. I just want to go home. This place is a fuckin' disgrace. Look at these bandages now. I've not seen a doctor in five days! I'm just lying here without an ear!"

The way he said it made us laugh, even Andy.

"What about money, Andy?" Julian asked him.

"I was hoping the British Consulate would help me. Ian was supposed to go but he's let me down. Would you two go for me?"

We could hardly say no.

"Where is it?" I asked.

"Here in Heraklion somewhere...."

"Find out for us when we come back tomorrow, and we'll go on Monday."

Mon 4th Sept.

We drove around Heraklion all day, negotiating its chaotic traffic and hot-headed drivers, following the different sets of directions that were given to us until finally we found the Embassy.

We entered the grand entrance way and asked to speak to the Consulate.

We sat waiting for ages until a middle-class, middle-aged woman led us through to be greeted by another middle-class, middle-aged woman, who looked at us bordering on contempt.

"I was wondering if you could help us," I started to explain. "Our friend was attacked and had his ear bitten off. He's in hospital in Heraklion and doesn't have any money to get home. We were wondering if you could possibly help us by arranging some sort of transportation?"

"Do you not have any money?" she looked down her nose at me, then at Julian.

"No. We are all working but don't have enough for a flight. We all plan on getting our last week's wages and going home on the 'Magic Bus.'"

"Can't your friend go by bus?"

"I think a three-day bus journey might be a little bit too much for him given his condition."

"In what way?" she intoned disdainfully, unemotional and cold.

"Well, he seems to still be in shock and I think a three-day bus journey would be too arduous for him."

"When did all this happen, exactly?"

"Five days ago."

"And he's still in shock?! Not able to take a bus journey, you hypothesise?"

"Well, obviously I'm not a doctor, and my prognosis could be unqualified, but seeing as he hasn't seen a doctor at the hospital for the five days he's been there, I can't give you a more accurate one. I can tell you though, with some certainty, that he is weak and upset, and doesn't have an ear, never mind his faculties. Who would look after him? What about food for three days?"

The two women started talking simultaneously, then spoke interacting. "You could certainly buy fruit and nuts." Switch.

"And sandwiches." Switch.

"And take bottled water..." Ready to switch.

"Look," I interrupted, "He doesn't have any money to travel, let alone sustain himself on your picnic for three days. Then there is the ten-hour coach trip from London to Edinburgh. He isn't Compos Mentis. I think he's in shock."

"I don't understand why you keep saying that he is in a state of shock."

"Well how would you feel if you had gotten your ear bitten off in a street fight, taken to Hospital in a taxi, holding your ear in your hand, then had it stitched back on without and anaesthetic and there are dead bodies lying in the corridor around you and cats in the ward?!"

"I feel that I could handle it quite well."

I laughed out loud. "You think that you could handle it quite well?!"

Blank stares. Their indifference was slightly disconcerting.

"Look, can you help us?" I tried.

"We can only act in an advisory capacity..." Switch.

"Couldn't you have a whip round?"

Julian cut right back, "Would you like to contribute?"

"Well..." she stammered.

"Well? Why exactly are you here?" Julian continued.

"Well, if people steal and they get caught they should go to prison..." she started to say.

"What's that got to do with us?" Julian interrupted her. "So you can't and won't help us get a British subject back to England?"

Blank stares.

"So, you're really just political figureheads then. I thought the Consulate was supposed to look after one of its own," Julian went on.

"If you object to the extent of our duties, I suggest you take it up with Mrs Thatcher."

"Fuck off!" We were in unison this time, getting up and walking out. It was the only thing said during the entire conversation that made sense. They seemed pointless. They had looked down on us like we were scum before we even opened our mouths. Our parting statement obviously confirmed it for them.

I just wondered what their kind of world must be like.

We came out of the Embassy feeling deflated, somehow feeling that we'd let Andy down.

"What now?!" Julian asked so innocently. It was a classic in understatement as he looked at me expecting me to have the answer. We both just laughed.

We changed for work at Flash that night and met our new boss, Tony, and his two mates that ran the club with him, Manos and Costas. They turned up at 9 pm then left us in charge while they went for something to eat.

The minute they had gone, Julian nipped inside and helped himself to the seven-star Metaxa. We used to get free drinks, as part of the job, but normally only got to drink the three-star Metaxa. So, seven-star was a treat.

The drink made you more relaxed and less inhibited when trying to tout for custom as a 'Kamaki', so it was actively encouraged. As our wages had been cut from 4000 drachs to 3000, and Eva's place was costing us 1000 drachs per day each, the free drink saved us a fortune. Even though a beer at that time, was only 150 drachs, about 75p.

Anyway, Metaxa, a Greek Brandy, and coke was our tipple and although the drink was free you couldn't take the piss by drinking bottle after bottle. That's why Julian was quick to take advantage of the fact Tony wasn't there.

The drink also helped you to laugh off the insults and refusals to come in. It also made us more open with each other and helped to forge our friendship as it's easier to talk when you're half-cut. It aided in chatting up the girls and enabled a bit of banter with the groups of holidaying lads.

Julian had said that earlier on in the season Flash had been busy but now it was quiet, and it was up to us to get it full again.

Looking up the Beach road we stopped two girls coming down to towards us. They told us they were new arrivals from London. We tried to lure them in with the invitation of a free drink but maybe they sensed our desperation, however, they did promise to come back once they had eaten. As they continued on their way, I 'caught eyes' with one of them and got a nice inviting smile. I watched her disappear down the street, then Julian nudged me.

"Keep a look-out for Tony." He picked up our empty glasses and darted back inside the club.

He came back moments later carrying two schooners full and two bottles of beer.

"Here," he said smiling. "Save me a double journey." I put my beer bottle down and sipped at my Metaxa. "Fuck me Julian, did you put any coke in this?!"

"Yeah. Why? Is it too strong for you? I thought you Scotsmen were supposed to be 'ard drinkers?!" he said this from the corner of his mouth, emphasising his Manc accent.

"You've just met the exception." He laughed.

It was true I'd never been able to hold my drink.

"It's funny," he said, "me old man always said to me 'never trust a Scotsman. Especially a drunk one, they're dangerous.'"

He kept chuckling as if picturing the moment when his dad had passed on this pearl of wisdom to him.

He went on.

"And I said, right dad. And I was thinking, when the fuck am I going to meet a Scotsman?! Yet here I am."

I laughed. Not because the story was particularly funny, but because Julian's laugh was infectious.

We must have looked like two tits, to the passers by who were now streaming in their droves down the Beach road and deliberately avoiding Flash, with two buffoons pissing themselves laughing without exchanging a word.

We had a brilliant time that night until 10.30 pm. That's when Tony and co. returned. It was also our first introduction of Flash's new Dj, Ally.

The guy was a wank. He was forty-ish. Receding dark hair, tight denims, leather jacket and, sporting the fool-proof way to identify a tool, cowboy boots. Worse still, they had metal toe-caps. The only thing that salvaged any pride for him was the fact that he didn't get off a bus but arrived on an impressive Harley Davidson. Straight from the set of 'The Wild One'.

Most Greeks liked to own motorcycles of some description. It was the one thing they all aspired to. They ranged in affordability from the lowly chicken chasers, like Dave's, to the automatic scooters the tourists favoured, to the Vespas, to the trials bikes, to the upper echelons of the bike world, for them, a Harley or a high-powered BMW.

Julian knew a bit about bikes. He said he was 'mad keen' on them when he was younger, so he was suitably impressed by Ally's.

I knew nothing about bikes and cared even less, apart from the fact I'd almost killed myself three years earlier on a Suzuki RM250 motocross bike.

It did look like a nice bike, but I didn't give it a second glance. Ally took my disinterested look for jealousy and sneered at me. Thus, began, our mutual dislike of one another.

I don't know if Julian actually liked him or just humoured him. But he repeated to me Andy's words of caution, almost like a maxim, 'Kenny, don't mess with the Greeks. They all stick together'.

This was undeniable. I had after all experienced it first hand with the Geordies. And it was something that I greatly admired.

I've always valued friendship and expected loyalty from my friends. That's why I'd been inclined to help Tim, as he had helped me. It was also why I was aware of my debt to Julian, who had put up money for the apartment and bike, without hesitation.

People who are friends are meant to stick together and maybe if you are out drinking and see someone from your area, you will help them out, but other than that, if there are a group of people fighting in the street or a club, you're not prompted to jump in just for your particular ethnic group. So, I did admire that about the Greeks.

From what I'd seen they were brave, but I think part of that came from knowing that tourists were well aware of them sticking together and this made tourists reluctant rather than scared to get involved against them, cos individually they didn't strike me as being much at all.

Wank, is what Ally most definitely was, but I would have cause to thank him one night when he helped me.

Even though he was a complete tit, it was hard to take the piss out of him because he spoke almost perfect English, although he did have an annoying habit of spouting Americanisms, 'fuck you and the horse you rode in on!' for example, but some of his lines were straight out of Brando films, who he obviously adored. But I was a Brando lover too, so recognised his lines and the movies they came from.

One phrase he was most fond of was, 'Take a flying fuck at a rolling doughnut.' straight out of Last Tango in Paris.

He would litter the conversations with the words, 'asshole' 'bullshit' and 'motherfucker'.

I think it came from the fact that they watched a lot of American films with stars like Chuck Norris, and Sly Stallone. I guess that's why they thought cowboy boots were cool.

All the Greek guys who loved themselves, the modern-day Adonis's, wore them with tight fitting denims. The sign of an arse back home, but, 'big time Johnny Potato' over here.

Another American habit that they had adopted was a fondness for Zippo lighters. Nearly all the Greek men smoked. So, they used to snap them open and light up by snapping their fingers against the flint wheel.

Guess what? Ally smoked, Marlboro, and he had a Zippo.

He used to sit outside Flash talking to us, sitting astride his Harley, side-on. One trouser leg ever so slightly pulled up just enough to reveal he was wearing cowboy boots, Marlboro in the side of his mouth, eyes slightly squinting as he talked to us through a plume of smoke.

A horse's cock personified.

He made our task impossible. I mean, we were trying our hardest to attract people in. trying to convince them, with our rhetoric, that Flash was THE club in town and here was this unfashionable cunt.

Julian and me, used to try and carry on with girls.

"Hiya girls, ladies," whichever, depending on their ages.

"Come try Flash. First drink free. Half price drinks 'til twelve, cocktails, as told by Kenny..."

With a fair amount of success. But every now and then, Ally butted in with those embarrassing Americanisms. The worst being when groups of guys passed telling us to 'fuck off' as they'd 'been in last night' and 'it was shit'.

We had no answer. We knew it to be true. But not Ally.

"Up yours, motherfucker! Fuck you and the horse you rode in on! Assholes! Sonsabitches!" he would scowl at them. "Go take a flying fuck at a rolling doughnut!"

Mercifully they knew he was Greek. Or we would have had trouble every night.

As the streets became busier and the girls passed in groups of three's and fours, dressed up, in short skirts and tight tops. Ally pulled out his Zippo. My heart sunk.

Fuck me.

"Ally, what time do you start Dj'ing?!" I would ask.

He would smile smugly at me.

"Plenty of time, my friend. Hey ladies, Flash discotheque. Free drinks first, half-price twelve, cocktails..."

Our lines lost something in his translation.

Julian was starting to snigger. That was all I needed. Him to start laughing.

In my half-drunk state, my imagination was running wild. Praying Ally wouldn't start wheelie-ing up and down the street.

As if in answer to my prayers, the two London girls turned up.

"Hiya. Told you we'd come back. Bleedin' 'ell. You two look well gone!" said the one I'd 'caught eyes' with earlier.

She was right. We were pissed.

"What's your name?" I asked her.

"Julie." She smiled so sweetly.

"Come on." I took her hand, "I'll take you inside and get you your free drink."

She moved in close to me and I put my arms around their shoulders.

"Is it busy?" her pal asked.

I swaggered in like Tony Montana. Drunk. A girl on each arm and the music blasting.

The place was empty. Not one person.

Tony, the manager caught my eye. I ignored his look.

"Two glasses of champagne, Tony." I chanced it. Smiling brightly.

Tony had a slight stammer. Which because of his grasp of English made him sound almost charming. He did also have a happy disposition.

"Eh, eh Ke Ke Kenny." It sounded like he was searching for the English equivalent. "Are you, you, working tonight?!" His eyes panned the emptiness. The coloured squares of the dance-floor, flashing intermittently looked ridiculous in the vacuum.

Costas, big moody bastard that he was, glowered at me from behind Tony.

Manos appeared from behind me and tapped me playfully on the shoulder.

"Customers or hostages?!"

I liked Manos. Usually.

"Why are we not busy, Malaka?!" Costas growled at me.

"Ask your Dj, bam!"

Two could play his game.

Malaka, means wanker or arse. Anything derogatory really. The Greeks used it in conversation all the time. Playfully or as an insult. I knew fine well which context Costas was using it in.

So, I did the same with our offensive words, and made them sound like terms of endearment. Bam has virtually the same definition in Scots.

"Why? What is wrong with our DJ?!"

Oh, oh.

How could I tell him that his mate, Ally, was the biggest clown in Clownsville and make it sound like a term of endearment? With his cowboy boots, and faded jeans, and ridiculous Americanisms?

Costas was making his way towards me from behind the bar, to confront me. I looked at him as he approached. Faded jeans and cowboy boots.

"What is wrong with the Dj, Malaka?!" he spat out.

See? My position was impossible.

Costas was a big mean broody looking bastard. He was six feet four, without his cowboy boots. He was at least sixteen stones. I'm five feet eleven and eleven stones. He would be a handful. He was gruff and aggressive with most people.

Me? I seemed to bring out the worst in him.

Manos stepped in front of me and Costas, as he was making his way to the bar, and gently led Costas back, too easily, behind with him.

Ah. Hold me back, I'll kill him.

Now he was back behind the bar, Costas said loudly.

"What is wrong with the Dj, motherfucker?!"

I don't know if Costas knew I had him sussed, but I did.

"Tony," I said, ignoring Costas, "he should be in here playing his music, not his lighter."

Costas continued to glare at me, from behind the bar.

"Ni," Tony said. Which means yes. "Tell him to come inside."

The girls released me from their vice like grip and followed me outside. I shook my arms to get the circulation going.

"He's fakin' touchy that big geezer!" they exclaimed.

I loved the sound of their Cockney wide-girl accents, and Julie was so cute.

"Ally. Tony wants you inside." I couldn't help but smile.

Ally narrowed his eyes and flicked his cigarette into the street, pocketed his Zippo and dismounted his Harley. He only came up to my shoulder.

Aah. It was starting to make sense. The Napoleonic complex. Ally was pushing five feet six in his cowboy boots.

I looked down at him as he brushed past me.

"Let's see if I can get this place rockin." He sauntered inside.

Julian started grinning. "He is a bit of an arse," he admitted.

"Just a bit."

"Look, we'll meet you later for a drink. This place is shit. Which is the best club?" Julie asked.

"Krpyton."

"Right. I'll see you there later." She smiled up at me warmly.

"Aye ok." I said, a little resigned.

She leant up and kissed me.

"Later." Then they turned and headed off down the street. Julian and me, watched their arse's as they went.

"She's cute," I offered. "And her pal's nice."

Julian sipped at his Metaxa and grinned.

"Yeah."

The rest of the night passed without incident and we managed to get Flash busier, well, busier than Dave had. Julian pissed off with another girl just before closing and left me to go down to Krypton on my own.

Julie was there. Waiting for me.

When her mate saw that I was on my own, her face fell.

"Where's your mate?" Julie asked, handing me a beer.

"He had to go through to Hersonisos to see the boss."

Her pal tutted.

"He says we might lose our jobs if we don't get it busy." I thought on my feet.

"What would you do then?" Real concern.

"I don't know," I lied.

Julie and me really hit it off. Her pal was doing her best to spoil it for us though.

"Come on Julie, let's go back to the apartment, I'm tired," she kept moaning.

"You're on holiday." I tried to sound upbeat.

"Yeah, but I'm still fakin' tired." She made a face at me when Julie wasn't looking.

Mmm, the appeal of that cockney wide-girl charm was wearing off now.

"All right." Julie finally succumbed to her nagging.

Finally, her pal smiled.

"Will you walk me up to our apartment, Kenny?"

I would have walked her to Hersonisos.

Her pal's face fell again.

"Aye of course, Julie." I said triumphantly, putting my arms around her and pulling her close.

She was small and petite and just getting prettier and prettier.

She wrapped one of her arms around my waist, to the bottom of my back, and her other arm, she put across my stomach, fluctuating as we walked, brushing my groin area and back up to my stomach. I walked all the way up that road with a hard-on.

Her pal stormed ahead. Arms folded sternly across her chest and periodically telling us to 'stop fakin' about', 'get a move on' and 'urry up!'

I affected a slight limp to accentuate the walking motion, so that Julie could feel that I was hard, and her hand would brush against my crotch even more.

Occasionally we would stop, and kiss, and her hand would linger on me and I would lean into her, increasing the pressure. I would also keep one eye on her friend and kiss Julie all the more passionately as she watched and fumed.

As we passed Flash, I led Julie into the doorway for a longer petting session and let her release me and have a nice long rub in the relative darkness. She stopped me from going all the way. "Not here," she whispered in my ear, and I could smell her sweet breath tinged with alcohol, as I ejaculated all over Flash's entrance.

"Will you pair hurry the fack up?!" her pal interrupted us.

"Yeh, coming." Julie looked down at me drunkenly. Her little face lit up.

I love girls when they are slightly drunk.

The walk up the Beach road to their apartment in the old town must have seemed like an eternity to her pal, but to me and Julie, it just flew by.

When we reached their apartment, I pretended not to notice as her mate leant down beside a plant pot and pulled their key out, on an oversized keyring.

"How the fuck is that supposed to fit inside your pocket?!" she complained, whilst opening the door.

"You're really enjoying this holiday, aren't you?" I quipped.

She made yet another face at me as Julie stumbled past her and said to me at the same time, "Come in, Kenny."

It was my turn to make a face, of victory.

"Do you want some tea, Kenny?" Julie asked rinsing a cup.

"Fuckin' tea at this time?!" Her pal.

"Aye, please," I accepted, even though I didn't even want a cup, and breezed in and flopped down on one of two beds.

"That's mine!" the pal said icily.

"Shock." I muttered, getting up and sinking deeper into the other bed.

"Nice apartment and this bed is comfy..." I started to say.

"It's too small," the pal interrupted.

"It's not that small..." I tried.

"It looked bigger in the brochure, didn't it, Jules?"

Julie sighed and struggled on, determined to make the tea. "I'll do it Julie, you're pissed."

"Yeah I am," she said flopping down on the bed beside me. She kissed me, while I kept my eyes open to look over at her pal, to see her scowling back.

"You'd be here all night making this." She looked at me whilst milking the cups, "And I'm not having that!"

"Sugar?" Directed at me.

"Yes love." Julie giggled.

I laughed, just to annoy her pal.

"Please love." I added.

Julie burst out laughing.

"Oh, fakin' funny you two, pair of comedians".

"Lighten up," I said. "You're on holiday."

"Urgh," she groaned at me.

It was obvious that her pal wasn't going to stop complaining and Julie was at the sleepy drunk stage, so as the clock said 7 am, I decided I was for the off.

"Oh, see you." Julie tried to brighten up.

"See you later." I got up to go.

"Later." She managed.

"See you." I nodded cheerfully at her pal.

Daggers.

I still had a faint smile on my face as I made my way home.

The morning was hot and hazy. Somehow the early morning walks home felt better after a satisfying night. It can be the loneliest time in the world. The ninjas nodded knowingly as I passed by.

I had a spring in my step and last night's limp had completely disappeared. I crossed from the shaded part of the street into the sunshine, but as I was ready to enter Eva, I realised that I didn't have a key. Shit.

I climbed up on to the balcony, pulled down some towels, that were outside drying, made a pillow for my head and fell asleep in the shade.

Wed 6th Sept. – 1pm.

"Kenny!"

I opened my eyes to see Julian standing over me. He was laughing.

"What are you doing sleeping there?! Did she blow you out?!"

"You've got the key. Nah, her pal was pissed off that you never showed up. I got back here about 7 ish."

I got up and went for a shower.

"Hurry up, Kenny. We'll take the bike up into the mountains."

Music to my ears. Finally, I'd get a chance to see a bit more of Greece.

I put on a pair of shorts, clean T-shirt, gave my hair a quick towel dry and grabbed my Wayfarers.

Julian picked up his leather pouch. Took some money out, put on his Aviators and turned into Jim Morrison.

"Let's go."

'THE WORLD ON YOU DEPENDS, OUR LIFE WILL NEVER END.'

At that moment, as we pulled away on that tatty red Vespa, Julian and me became friends. The only ones in the world.

I felt like the sun was shining just for us.

The Vespa carried us out of Malia. He turned the bike onto the Mohos road. The road snaked upwards and around again, each level taking us higher and the view became greater. I looked down over Malia behind us, fading. I looked down and over at Stalis, watching the coastline curve towards Hersonisos, falling from seamless sea into endless sky.

We continued up.

We reached the point where Andy had stopped on my second day, that seemed to be the top. People had stopped and were taking pictures like we had done, as if this was the Zenith. The road did look like it stopped and blended into the hillside, and it was a decent vantage point, but Julian drove towards it and as we approached it, it opened up. Then it took a sharp arc downwards. We drove on and down. The scenery changed and grew greener and greener. A solitary goat stood out alone on the hillside.

"There's our kid," Julian commented.

It was the first words spoken in easily half an hour.

The comment came and went. Not out of place but not needing a reply. We drove on as the road flattened out into a long straight.

Everything now seemed natural, untouched.

Julian had the Vespa at full throttle, but we seemed to whisper through.

The road started to incline to the left and we turned a corner and found ourselves in an old town square. It just came upon us.

There were a few chairs outside a small café and a cigarette kiosk with an old man inside. It looked like something from the 1930's. An old truck lay motionless next to an old black-framed bicycle. Surreal. I don't know why but Julian drove around the square again as if unsure of what he had seen the first time. The man in the kiosk smiled at us. I knew Julian must be thinking the same as me. I couldn't see his eyes through his Aviators, but he just slowed the bike down on the second circuit as if we were travelling in slow motion. Magical.

He picked up the speed suddenly, interrupting my reverie, and drove out of the square and past a strange, somewhat out of place, new building, on our left. It was a school.

The road bent abruptly to our left and we drove through an olive grove. It was like an olive grove avenue, hanging over us protectively. We drove through it and up to the left as the road u-turned sharply. The bike laboured, and Julian dropped a gear and manoeuvred it expertly round the tight bend. We were off and climbing. Up and up. The road twisted and turned. This wasn't a hill it was a mountain.

Sharp twists in the road were met with bursts of speed from the bike as we continued our ascent.

On our right-hand side, from out of nowhere, completely out of place, was a tiny chapel. Standing alone and isolated.

As we passed, Julian slowed down so we had the time to take a look inside.

A small perfectly formed structure.

Inside a portrait of the Virgin Mary, hung on the wall. Next to it a crucifix. In front of them was a board for kneeling on.

The bike was struggling, on these sharp inclines, with both our weights to contend with. There wasn't any straight road to get up any speed.

We climbed a particularly steep incline and then the road opened up and we seemed to be at the bottom of a valley. To the right of us a field of tiny trees. Further over to our right were the mountain tops. We had climbed some distance. The air was perceptibly cooler but fresher and pure.

We were on a straight road bending ever so slightly to the left.

Up ahead of us overhanging a mountain was a monastery!

"Look at that!" Julian exclaimed.

It seemed to hang as if suspended in the air. It was only on closer inspection that you could see it was attached to the rocks.

I swear time stood still.

Only the heat reminded me that I was here. Part of it all. Feeling alive in my time.

Julian continued on.

The road swept to our left, and weaved back up and over to our right, covered by the branches of over hanging trees. Shafts of spattered light pierced through the leaves. I put my sunglasses up onto my head, to take it all in, scared in case I might miss a single moment.

The road steepened further, and the bike laboured again. Julian pressed on without missing a beat.

The hum of the bike and the feeling of heat was intense as we were encapsulated in this essence of beauty.

The bike soared upwards. To the right, and into view through the branches, I caught a glimpse of a café. It was perched on high, on the right-hand side of the road as it flattened out slightly.

Julian pulled over, and we looked back the way we had come. We could now see the tops of the trees that had just provided shelter to us, back down into the valley with the perfect lines of tiny trees, now in infinite shades of green and framed with purple tinged mountains to the left.

We looked around the café. Five or six people, men and women, sat with bottles of beer smiling at us, as if sharing the same secret.

We approached the front door of the café, but at the side of the door, next to a large fridge, sat an old man with a gap-toothed smile. He motioned to a table perched on the ledge with a spectacular view of the valley below us.

"Two beers please." Julian nodded to him, signalling two with his fingers. We took our seats at the table.

"It's beautiful up here!" Julian said in awe.

I looked out across this stunning vista and didn't know what to say.

The old man appeared at our side. He placed three bottles of ice-cold beers on the table, condensation just beginning to trickle down the glass, flicked open the tops with his opener, handed one to each of us and one for himself, tapped his bottle against ours, smiled his charming gap-toothed smile and said, "Hey, there you are."

I swear I've never had a colder bottle of beer or one that tasted better.

"This is how I'd like to feel all the time." Julian sipped down his bottle. "Perfect."

The old man brought over another three bottles. Clicked them against ours and took away the empties, smiling.

We gazed out before us, drinking down our beers, caught perfectly in time.

'WOULDN'T IT BE GREAT IF IT WAS LIKE THIS ALL THE TIME?'

Julian pushed his chair back, got up, and as usual, went to pay. I got up and savoured the view for a few more seconds, committing it to memory. As I turned away from the table and made my way to the bike, I caught sight of the old man warmly shaking Julian's hand and covering it with his own. They exchanged words. He waved over at me and smiled.

We got on the bike, turned back to wave, but the old man was gone.

Julian sped off adjusting his position on the bike and changing gear at the same time.

We drove on, dream-like, for the next few miles. The road reaching forever upwards. A white road sign appeared. The first one I can recall seeing: LASSITHNI PLATEAU 7.

I began to feel excited, butterflies in my stomach. We climbed and soared. Wishing I could put it to music.

The road cleared out into a straight and we found ourselves between two mountains. The road rose upwards to the left and there it was, LASSITHNI PLATEAU.

I didn't think that anything could better the view at the café. This did.

Between the peaks of two mountains, at the earth's summit, it felt like to me. There, lying before us, was a valley of such sweet beauty.

I could never do the view or this feeling justice.

We climbed off the bike and stumbled on to look. It seemed almost untouchable, unreachable. It lay there in complete perfection. We just looked on. Yearning.

I knew that I'd never see it again. Or feel this good again. I experienced a real moment of clarity.

We looked at each other and back. Turning around full circle, like we had in the village square.

Standing there, for a few fleeting moments. Knowing it couldn't last. Hands on hips, eyes glazed. It was there at Lassithni Plateau, that I saw all that there is.

I don't know what compelled us to leave and get back on the bike, but we did. As we drove back down and round, we seemed to be winding down from our high, with the road.

So did the view. Gradually decreasing. Winding us ever so gently back down.

"Do you want a shot of the bike, Kenny? So, I can have a smoke?" Julian asked, kind of bringing us back to reality.

"I'm hopeless on a bike, Julian. I had a bad crash on one once."

"It's mostly downhill now. Just take it easy," he said, pulling the bike over.

"Are you sure?!"

"Look. Just pull this clutch lever in with your left hand and push this bit around."

The gears were indicated 1,2,3,4 on the handlebars. With a line to indicate what gear you were in. Simple.

Julian fished out a cigarette, lit it, pulled on it deeply a few times, and said, "Let's go."

I got on, then he got on. I hesitated. Taking my time selecting a gear.

"Come on! You're like an old woman!"

I pulled in the clutch. Put it forward into first gear.

"Ease the clutch out..." Julian started to say as I pulled away swaying all over the road.

"Take it easy!" He roared. "Whoa!"

I tried hard to steady the bike which was whining noisily.

"This is not too bad," I said confidently.

"Well for fucksake put it in second gear before the engine blows!"

"Oh right," I said sheepishly.

I moved slowly through the gears as we rolled easily down the hill. I felt good now. Driving the bike with the wind in my face, blowing my hair back.

We passed the little chapel again and I shakily rounded the sharp corner. The road dropped down steeply. Up ahead was the ridiculously sharp u- bend that descended into the olive grove.

I started to lose control of the bike. The road was coming up too fast. I tried to brake and knocked the gears into neutral. We were still free-wheeling too fast. I just steered by instinct.

"Geronimo!" I shouted, as we hurtled downwards, perilously close to the edge and a sheer drop.

"Geronimo!" Julian roared beside me, thinking I was losing control also.

"Geronimo!" We both bellowed, as the road steepened and I wrestled with the steering, with the bike heading towards the olive trees.

I don't know how I managed to manoeuvre the bike around that tight u- bend without us hitting anything or falling off, but I did.

The second the bike straightened up and we came to an abrupt halt, Julian leapt of the bike and started laughing with relief.

I let the bike fall gently on its side and stepped away, flopping down against an olive tree.

"Don't let me drive a bike again, Julian."

He dropped down against the tree opposite me.

"Don't worry. I won't!" His Manchester accent strained with laughter.

"I'm a nervous wreck. Look," I said placing my hand out in front of me.

"But it's straight as anything," he said, stopping laughing.

"Aye, but I brake with this one," I said, bringing up my shaking left hand.

Julian burst out laughing, rolling around on his back.

"Haven't you seen Blazing Saddles?!" I asked.

"No." He kept on laughing.

I caught him looking at the large scar down my arm.

"How did you get that?!" he stopped laughing.

"I had a motorbike crash, about three years ago."

"What happened?"

"A mate of mine bought a motocross bike..."

"Oh, they're lethal them. What kind was it?"

"RM 250."

"They're really quick."

"They can wheelie in fourth gear."

"Oh yeah, I know."

"Anyway, to cut a long story short. I asked for a go. SPLAT!"

"What did you hit?!"

"A wall!"

"Fuckin' 'ell!"

"Smashed my arm and my leg, broke a few ribs."

"How long were you in hospital for?"

"Six months."

"Six months?! Andy's moaning about five days!"

"It is hardest at first." I recalled.

Julian drew on his cigarette.

"What's that lump on your wrist?"

"Skin graft."

"Where from?"

"My thigh."

I hitched up my shorts a little and showed him a square patch on my right thigh, slightly lighter in colour.

"What did they do with that?"

"The bone had come through my wrist. Compound fracture, it's called. So, they used this skin to cover it. The worst bit was having it stitched to my stomach for three weeks until the graft takes." I lifted up my T-shirt to show him my scar.

"Fuckin' 'ell! I bet that hurt!"

"Only when I laughed."

Julian laughed at this.

I don't know why I told him so much. I hadn't shared any of this with anyone else.

"No, I'm serious," I told him. "That's when it hurt the most. The guy whose bike it was used to visit me in hospital. They three weeks were a nightmare. He was trying to cheer me up one day and said, 'one day you'll look back on this and laugh about it'. No me, I said, I'll never laugh again, he's never let me forget it."

The day was turning to evening as we sat there laughing in the olive grove. Picking up and eating the odd olive or throwing them at the bike.

The sky was all different colours but mostly it basked us in a magnificent orange glow.

"We'd better get back and get changed for Flash." Julian started up the Vespa.

"Fuck Flash," I muttered, climbing on the back.

"Fuck them and the Vespa they came riding in on!" Julian said pulling away, shooting as straight as an arrow, whilst changing gear and adjusting his seating position.

"Assholes!" I shouted.

"Sonsabitches!" We chorused.

When we got back to the apartment to change for work, we still seemed on a high. So, we dressed in smarter clothes than usual. Julian put on a pair of black semi-flared pinstripe trousers, black palladiums and borrowed my white dress shirt.

I put on a pair of white needle-pin Levi cords and borrowed Julian's white and pink flower pattern shirt and my desert boots. We were determined to get Flash busy. We dabbed a spot of aftershave. Fahrenheit for him, which I hated, and Kouros for me. That was us ready. Dynamite.

By the time, Tony, Manos and Costas left us at 9.30 pm and came back at 10.30 pm. We were pissed. The club was filling up nicely but hardly anyone was dancing. Julian went over to Ally in his booth and got him to play his favourite record, 'Humanoid', 'Stakker Humanoid'. Julian glided off around the dance floor. Dancing better than that night in Krypton.

All eyes were on him as he moved. Lads watching. Women watching. An older couple in their forties watched on, the lady staring at Julian, unable to take her eyes off him. She was mesmerised, her eyes full of lust. I expected her husband to react jealously, but he just looked on resigned.

Julian was in a world of his own.

The dance floor filled up around him. When his song stopped, he stopped dancing abruptly, and just walked off the floor.

By twelve o'clock Flash was busy. The busiest I'd seen it. Of course, Ally took the credit.

Every time, me or Julian escorted a group of girls in for their free glass of champagne. Ally looked across at us from his booth, spread his hands out to sweep across the dance floor and winked at us. Then he continued to clap his hands and shuffle his feet, snapping his fingers, completely out of time with the music. Wank.

The London girls didn't pass that night. Which was fine with me as Flash was full of good-looking girls and we had 'caught eyes' with several.

Later on, about 1 am, the girl from the hospital, who was looking after Andy came to see us.

She was small and dark-skinned with a lovely open smile, but strange glazed over eyes. She told us that Andy was getting out of hospital the following day.

I don't know who she was or where she came from, but she was good to Andy.

I don't know why we didn't go home with any girls that night. There were plenty of offers. Maybe it was because we were spoiled for choice and couldn't make up our minds.

We even managed to persuade guys who had told us to 'fuck off' before to come in and try Flash now.

We laughed and joked our way through the night until it was 3 am. Both drunk, we decided on a Souvlaki, a Greek kebab, and home.

"Kenny!"

I heard Julian's voice from afar.

"Come on! Wake up! We've got to leaflet the beach!"

"No!" I pulled my bed sheet over my head.

"Come on, arse. Get up!"

"Why don't we just pay Dave to do it?!"

"Yeah right. But we have to get up and find him first!" Julian was lying back in his bed blowing smoke up into the air.

I raised my head and called through the dividing door. "What time is it?!"

"Noon."

"Plenty of time."

"If we get down and do it now, we can get something to eat then a few hours kip before work. If Andy gets out today, he'll want to go out tonight."

"Maybe."

I got up and put a pair of shorts and trainers on.

"Do you think Andy'll go home?" Julian asked.

"I don't know. Probably."

"What about money?"

I shrugged my shoulders, "Do you want anything from the shops?"

"Yeah, get me a coke."

As I was coming back from the shop, carrying two cans of coke, Julian was coming down the stairs.

"Here's your sunglasses," he handed them to me as I passed him a can.

"Ta."

Julian drove the bike and drank from his can at the same time, making it look ridiculously easy.

"I might have another go at this bike later." I stated.

He didn't reply.

When we got to Flash, Tony was there waiting for us.

"Eh, eh, so, so, you ARE going to leaflet the beach today?!" he smiled.

We didn't reply, just took the flyers off the bar and turned to go.

Tony called after us. "When you have finished leafleting the beach, come back to Flash. We are having a smoke."

"Yeah?!" Julian's face lit up. He grabbed the flyers from me and once outside said. "It'll be easy handing these out today. We won't get no crap cos it was busy last night."

I hated doing this. It was far too hot to be walking about a beach.

Julian had a spring in his step though. He whizzed through his bundle.

"C'mon Kenny!" He hurried me, grabbing a bunch of flyers, "Let's be 'aving you!"

Whilst we were handing out the leaflets, in our haste, we just caught a glimpse of two young girls eyeing us coquettishly.

They were sunbathing with their parents and younger siblings. They looked familiar.

It's the two girls we took home from Krypton. We smiled and walked away quickly.

"Fuckin' 'ell!" Julian exclaimed, "They look different during the day! How old do you think they are?!"

I took a quick glance back. "Old enough!" I hoped.

We were done and back inside the welcome cool of Flash within half an hour.

"You are ke, ke, keen, Julian, eh?" Tony smiled, and he rolled the strangest looking joint I'd ever seen. He used about twelve skins as he expertly rolled and licked a huge cornet shaped joint.

"Roll one while we wait, Julian." Manos nodded at Julian passing him the cigarette papers.

He didn't need a second invitation as he made a three skinner in double quick time. He helped himself to a large amount of grass, from the big bag on the table.

Costas got up from the table and went behind the bar. "Drinks, Malaka's?!" he asked us grudgingly.

At least he was consistent.

"Coke, arse." From me.

"I'll have a beer please." Julian said, lighting up. He drew on it deeply and blew on the end of the tip. "It's nice that," he said, passing the joint to Manos. Julian's expertise seemed to meet with their approval.

"Here." Costas handed Julian his beer.

"Ta."

"Malaka." He tapped my shoulder with my bottle of coke.

"Tit." I cheerfully accepted it.

Tony finally finished his creation. He lit it and drew on it sharply several times, before passing it to me.

"No thanks, Tony. I don't smoke."

Tony looked surprised. Costas groaned, liking me even less. He reached across my chest to take the joint from Tony.

"You, you don't, eh, smoke?" Tony asked. I shook my head.

"Why?!" Costas, accusingly.

"I just don't. That's all."

"It's unusual." Manos passed Julian's joint to Tony. "Most Greeks smoke. Even cigarettes."

"Aye, I've noticed that." I nodded. "But I don't smoke cigarettes and I don't like grass or hashish."

"Have you tried it before?" Tony asked.

"Aye. Maybe it's because I don't smoke cigarettes, that smoking it, just makes me feel sick, who knows?"

I wasn't about to explain that I thought cannabis smokers were bams. Especially the ones I knew from back home. Thinking that they were somehow tapped in to a higher force or on a deeper spiritual plane than me. That they felt music more than me. Thought more profoundly. Show me a cannabis smoker, I'll show you a bam. I looked at Costas. Point made.

"You have to go through that sick stage, Malaka." From Costas.

Wise words.

"Nah, it's not for me." I sipped from my drink. I watched them passing the two joints back and forward to each other and noticed the different mannerisms they had for holding and inhaling.

Not much was happening in terms of conversation. Just the odd contented smile. The Greeks spoke occasionally to each other in Greek.

Yeh, a higher plane.

"Can we put some music on?" Julian asked.

"Ni, ni." Tony nodded yes. He got up and walked over to the Dj box and plugged in the power.

Could I rig that to electrocute, Ally?

"Help yourself. But not, not, too loud."

Ally had some good records surprisingly. Julian put on Marvin Gaye, 'What's Going On', and returned to the table.

We sat there for at least an hour. Me feeling slightly out of place. Not tapped in to their ethereal plane.

"Come on Julian, let's get something to eat," I said finally.

"In a bit."

"You stay here then. I'm off. Give me the key."

"Hang on a bit..."

"Nah. You stay here as long as you like. It just doesn't appeal to me mate."

"Right." He gave me the key, "See you in a bit."

"I'll get some rolls and cheese and take them back to the apartment."

"Yeah, ta."

I turned right as I came out of Flash. Walked down and then turned left, up towards the Galaxy bar.

"Kenny!"

I turned as I heard my name.

I looked to see Dave's big ugly face.

"Andy's out of hospital. I've just seen him. He's got a big bandage on his ear!"

"Where is he?"

"He was in Hersonisos this morning. He says that he's going home."

"Was he alright?"

"He seemed right pissed off."

Dave's voice sounded very effeminate sometimes. He came from Warrington, Cheshire, which is about half-way between Manchester and Liverpool. So, depending on what company he was in, his voice switched between the two cooler accents.

If he spoke with a scouse accent though, which he seemed to prefer, in front of Scousers, they would ask which part of Liverpool he was from. When he said Warrington, they picked up on it and asked why he spoke with a scouse accent when he was from nowhere near Liverpool. People from Manchester did the same thing to him. So, when he wasn't sure where you were from, he spoke with this stupid in-between accent. Which was actually his own.

Everybody liked Dave. Except me. He tried to be everyone's friend. 'Dave's a nice guy,' they all said.

All the girls used him as a shoulder to cry on when they had been treated badly by a boyfriend.

He used to mistake this for them fancying him. 'Dave, I like you as a friend' was something he heard quite a lot.

I hated him. He was a big, smelly, long greasy-haired, galoot. He was a bit over six feet tall, gangly and hunch shouldered, with an enormous jaw and over-sized teeth, set in a permanent stupid smile.

He was harmless enough, but he was always coming up to our apartment and 'borrowing' things. I hate selfish people who don't pull their weight.

He never washed his clothes. He just changed them every couple of nights and sprayed them with our aftershaves. He'd 'borrow' hair wax, gel, soap, razors, deodorant and especially our aftershaves.

It really annoyed me.

"Will you do the beach for us?" I asked him, though.

"Yeah. No problem."

"Right. Ta. See you later." He got up, to follow me.

"Where are you going?" he asked.

"Up for a sleep before work," I said, sharply.

"Oh right." He sat down again.

"Where's Julian then?"

"Dunno." I shrugged, walking on and turning onto the main road.

I stopped at one of the mini-markets and got four rolls, some sliced cheese, two cokes and a bottle of water. I crossed the road to Eva. As soon as I opened the apartment door, the heat hit me, like walking into an oven.

I put the food down on Julian's double bed and opened the balcony doors. A cool breeze filled the room. I opened up the dividing doors also. I was half way through a cheese roll when I fell back against my bed and drifted off to sleep.

"Kenny! All I seem to do is wake you up. If it wasn't for me, you'd miss the whole time here!" Julian was shaking my mattress with his foot.

The room was dark.

"Come on. It's 10 pm. I came back and crashed out too."

I pulled on a pair of jeans, sprayed on some deodorant and put on a clean T-shirt.

"You're getting as bad as Dave!" Julian quipped as I splashed some water on my face.

I sprayed myself with aftershave.

"Do you think?!" I yawned.

"How come you're tired?! You've done fuck all!" Julian shook his head, smiling. "I didn't get out of that opium den till 5.30 pm. I don't remember driving home or what made me wake up. I was proper licked."

We brushed our teeth and drove to Flash.

Tony, Manos and Costas were late as well. They all arrived grinning, except Costas, but at least he wasn't scowling for once.

"Ev, ev, everbody sleepy?" Tony joked.

The night dragged. Nobody could be bothered. Except Ally.

Andy turned up looking better than ever.

"How are you, young gun?" I asked.

"I feel shit Kenny. They've stitched my ear back on. How does it look?" He said this as if he had no recollection of telling us at the hospital.

He gently pulled back what I can only describe as looking like a single ear-muff.

Half of his ear, from top to bottom, was jet black. It didn't look good. "They're hoping it's going to take. What do you think?"

"I don't know, Andy." I tried to sound hopeful too. "It's hard to tell." The stitches, congealed blood, swelling and bruising didn't help.

"What are you going to do?" Julian asked, a bit casually.

"I don't know, Jules." Andy looked down at his feet, sighing. "Have you got any fags?"

"Yeah."

Julian took three cigarettes from his packet. Put one behind each ear, lit one and handed the rest of the packet to Andy, "Take these."

Andy took a cigarette from the packet and Julian lit it for him.

"It's a good thing you gave me the packet," he said, looking at the cigarettes behind Julian's ear. "I won't be keeping mine there again!"

We all laughed. Andy was good at self-deprecating humour. Thankfully.

"Have you had anything to eat?" I asked him.

"Not for two days."

"What about that young girl?" Julian asked him.

"If it wasn't for her bringing me sandwiches and milk and biscuits, I would have been in that corridor with the rest of the dead bodies."

Julian handed Andy 1000 drachs. "Go and get some Souvlakis for us."

"Get me a beer from Flash, Kenny," Andy said, walking away, "I'll be back in a minute."

Andy came back, and we ate our kebabs and spoke about what he was going to do. He was pissed off about having to go home.

"I'll have to," he said, "to get my ear fixed."

"What about money?" I asked.

"I met this bird in Hersonisos that I know. She's going to give me £150 for a flight. I've got to go through and meet her tonight."

He stayed for a couple of more hours before leaving for Hersonisos, saying he would meet us later in Krypton.

The night was really dragging for some reason. Even the streets were pretty quiet.

Just when I thought things couldn't get any worse, Julian looked across at me over his glass of Metaxa.

"Kenny," he said, nodding his head down the street. "Isn't that your bird?!" Julian grinned, still behind his glass.

I turned around and saw Julie walking up the other side of the road. Hand in hand with some twat. Her pal, who was also hand in hand, smirked over at me as they passed.

Julie caught my eye and offered a meek apologetic look.

"Finally got yourself a man I see," said Julian, gesturing over with his head to her pal. "It only took you eleven days!" he added.

Her face went bright red. I didn't even bother to look at Julie's reaction. Now I knew why I hadn't seen her though. My mind was made up.

Julian stuck his tongue into his bottom lip and said in his best Albert Steptoe voice, "She's blown you out!"

I couldn't help but laugh.

"At least we know our next mission." I said.

Julian kept laughing. "What, if you can't shag' em, rob 'em?!"

"It's a pity," I mused. "She was a nice girl."

"Everybody say aah."

Fri 8th Sept.

Andy woke us up. He came crashing in carrying rolls and crisps and juice.

"And a wee bar of chocolate for you, Kenny," he said sarcastically throwing me a Bounty.

"Cheers, young gun."

"Do you fancy going down the beach today, Andy?" Julian asked him.

"I've got to keep my ear covered from the sun," he said, pointing at his bandage in the mirror. "And there's no way I'm sitting on the beach wearing an ear-muff!"

We all laughed.

"I was going to sunbathe on the roof." He opened the balcony door and started climbing up onto the roof.

"Pass me up the towels and the rolls and stuff, Kenny," he shouted down to me.

I started passing the stuff up as Julian climbed up.

"Here, I got the papers." Andy handed me a copy of The Sun, took The Daily Record for himself and said to Julian, "I got you The Mirror."

"Cheers Andy."

"And I got some batteries for that radio cassette too."

We stayed on the roof all day. Andy was in good spirits and cracking jokes.

It must have felt good for him to be out of hospital. Back with his mates again, basking in the sun, topping up his tan! We spent the day reading bits aloud from our newspapers and listening to music, at last.

"Why do you sometimes call each other 'young gun'?" Julian asked.

"The guy who runs our local pub, 'The Artful Dodger' Davy, calls us it when we go there. So, it just kind of stuck and sometimes we call each other it," Andy explained.

"Is that why you call each other 'arse' all the time as well?"

Andy laughed. "That's just to emphasise your point, sometimes. Like when the Greeks say malaka. We just say arse, eh, Kenny?"

"Aye." Pause. "Arse."

Andy flicked a piece of his roll at me, "And the fact that he is an arse!"

"I just wondered. Sometimes it sounds as though you really mean it."

"We do!" we chorused.

The day passed quickly, and we climbed down the roof and got ready for work.

Andy came down to Flash with us and we all drank until Tony, Manos and Costas came back. Then Andy left for Hersonisos, saying he would see us later in Krypton.

Julian slipped away about 11 pm. He was back by 11.30 pm and nobody even noticed he had gone.

"I stashed the stuff at the banana plantations."

"What did you get?!"

"A little bit of money, some travellers, a camera. Not much. Here," he said reaching in to his pocket. "I got you a pair of Julie's knickers. At least you'll be able to get into them now!" He burst out laughing.

About 1 am, Julian spotted the London girls walking up the Beach road, on the other side again.

Julie glanced furtively over, and I pretended not to notice. Julian deliberately made a point of smiling at them.

I stopped two girls and tried to charm them into Flash. I could feel Julie's mate laughing as the two girls gave me a wide berth and kept on walking.

"Nice one, Kenny!" Julian remarked. "She'll think you're a right arse now!" He emphasised the arse.

"Oh, I notice you've caught on quick to us calling each other arse then?!"

"Yeah. I could get quite used to it. Arse!"

"You're pissed I see!"

"Yeah I am. I don't know why, I haven't had that much to drink. Must be that 'mission' that's put me in a good mood. I see you're holding yours better now."

The saying 'mission' came from the Rebel MC song, Just Keep Rockin', which was popular at that time and had the line 'get funky I'm on a mission'. So, it became our song and phrase.

I made to go inside, "Do you want another drink, Julian?"

"Yeah. Cheer up, Kenny, there's plenty more fish in the sea." He came over and put his hand on my shoulder, "Plenty more pebbles on the beach."

"I've seen Rising Damp, Julian!" I ducked under his arm and darted into Flash.

When I came back outside, Julian was talking to Dave.

"Give us 1000 drachs, Kenny."

I put our drinks down to reach into my pocket and Dave picked one up.

"Can I have a sip of that?" He already had.

I took my drink from his hand and handed him the 1000 drachs with the other. As I put my mouth to the glass, I said to Dave, "Which side did you drink out of?!"

"Aah, fuck off." He half-laughed in his effeminate accent.

Julian laughed into his drink, spilling some.

"Do you want me to do the beach tomorrow as well?" Dave asked.

Dave liked handing out the flyers as it gave him an opportunity to talk to girls and let people see what a 'nice guy' he was.

"Yeah. We can't be arsed with it," Julian said.

"I don't mind it me. The extra money is handy. Especially for an hour's work."

"An hour?!" Julian exclaimed. "We do it in twenty minutes! Here, here, here." He gestured with his hands "We don't even talk to birds unless they're stunners."

"I like it 'cos you get to see all the nice-looking birds first," Dave went on.

"And get the first knock backs from them!" I chipped in.

"Do you get much stick from the lads?" Julian asked.

"A bit. Most of them know I don't work on the door now. If they do start on me, I just say that I only hand out the leaflets and don't work on the door anymore. Then they usually say that you two are a pair of cheeky cunts!"

We both laughed.

Dave continued, mimicking other people, saying "Right pair of cheeky twats. They're always pissed and laughing at something."

Then he had the cheek to ask us, "How come it's so quiet?"

"You worked here when it was quiet, Dave. You tell us?!" I said.

"Costas blames Kenny," Julian cut in.

"Which one is Costas?" Dave asked.

"The big moody bastard!" I cut in.

"I dunno why it's quiet," said Julian. "Krypton was shit when we first came here, and Flash was busy. Look at it now. You know how it goes, Dave. It could be because they've got the best Dj's now. All them Yanks from the Air-Force base. We've got Ally!"

"You don't have any missions lined up do you?" Dave enquired.

"Nah," I stated flatly.

"Give us a shout if you do. I could do with the extra cash."

"What do you spend it all on, Dave?! Not toiletries that's for sure!"

"Aah, fuck off, ya cheeky bastard." He half-laughed walking away.

"I don't know why you don't like him, Kenny. I think he's alright, me."

"He's a smelly bastard. That's why this place is dead. People thought it was Flash that stunk. It was him!"

"Yeah but other than that...?"

"He's always mooching stuff. 'Have you got a mission lined up?'," I mimicked his voice. "He's always on the scrounge, 'borrowing' things. I hate that!"

"He's harmless though."

"Aye, I know that. I don't pick on him 'cos he's a sap. I hate selfish people. They do fuck all and expect to share your things. Especially when we take all the risks. I hate his big stupid gormless face and permanently happy disposition. Trying to be everyone's pal. Dave the worker's pal. You can't be everyone's pal. He's what my auld man would call, a stumer."

"What's a stumer?!"

"Him!"

Julian smiled, "He's asked to move in with us if Andy goes home."

"No chance!"

"His money will help pay the rent," Julian teased.

"I'll do the beach if we need the money! He's got no chance of moving in with us! No way! No danger! No fuckin' way!"

"Are you sure?!"

Bang on 3 am we left Flash. Jumped on the Vespa and drove down the Beach road to the cross-roads half way down, turned right and headed for the banana plantations.

Julian drove up and down the street a few times. I thought to check that it was safe. Then...

"Kenny. I can't remember which one it is!" He burst out laughing, nearly losing control of the bike.

"Pull over!"

I climbed off the bike while Julian struggled to put it on its stand. He finally let it fall to the ground and collapsed alongside it in hysterics.

"Arse." I said, down at him.

He couldn't speak for laughing.

"Fuckin' arse." I repeated.

I looked along the road at all the banana plantations. There were scores of them. Each about the size of a football pitch. All covered in plastic sheeting, greenhouse shaped.

There was a road to our right which by-passed the Beach road and led directly on to the main road. Along the other side was the graveyard.

The continuation of this road led to the fabled German hotel that nobody had ever robbed. We'd prowled their grounds a couple of times, but they had a security guard who patrolled them, so we decided not to risk it and stick to easier targets, but it was frustrating thinking it was impossible for us.

"Which way did you come?" I asked hopefully, trying to jog his memory.

"Down past the graveyard," Julian said, getting to his feet.

"Right." He paused. "It's one of those ones. Definitely." He pointed at a row of about fifteen plantations. They were basically each a huge plastic tent set in a field to grow bananas and to be fair to him they all looked identical.

"Come on," he chirped. "Let's go."

We wheeled the bike off the road out of sight and crawled on our hands and knees through the dirt fields. We lifted the plastic up around each greenhouse and felt around inside.

Ten plastic tents later. Julian found the bag he'd stashed.

He turned to face me in the moonlight. All I could see on his black muddy face was his white teeth smiling triumphantly.

"Told you I'd find it!"

I shook my head.

"Do you fancy going for a drink?!" he asked, deadpan.

We crept out of the field towards the Vespa, but we needn't have worried, the road was deserted and only a few lights shone from within the grounds of the German Hotel.

Sneaking back into Pension Eva, we took off our filthy clothes and rinsed them in the shower to remove as much dirt as possible before stuffing them in to a bag.

"I'll take them to the launderette first thing in the morning," Julian offered.

I opened the balcony door to let some fresh air in. Then I opened the bag to see what we had. I pulled out £75 in English money. £150 of traveller's cheques and a nice camera worth about £80.

Good. The travellers were only signed with the girl's first initial. So, no way to tell if they were male or female names. It mostly didn't matter as the Greeks weren't too familiar with a lot of English names and their respective spellings.

I put the money in my drawer. Next to my last English £20. I then put the camera and travellers back in the bag and threw them up onto the roof.

Then I flopped down on my bed. Julian was already sound asleep on his.

Sat 9th Sept.

"Kenny!" Julian shouted through the partition at me, "Get up!"

I looked up to see Dave helping himself to a lump of hair wax.

"Go easy with that Dave!" I yelled at him.

He half laughed nervously. Then he sprayed himself from top to bottom with Fahrenheit. Even though I hated the Fahrenheit. I hated Dave more.

I got up.

"Go easy with that you!" I grabbed it from his hand.

"You's two are filthy! What have you been doing?" Dave looked at us.

"We wiped ourselves on one of your tops thinking it was a towel!" I said, sarcastically.

Julian, who was lying on his bed smoking said,

"Dave? Do you want to earn some money?"

"Yeah!" Dave turned to face him, then gormlessly asked, "How much?"

Julian must have gotten the bag down as it was lying on the table.

"Give him the travellers cheques, Kenny. We've got £150 worth of those. If you cash them for us and take that camera to the shop in

Hersonisos, you can keep what you get for it. Oh, and dump that bag while you're through there."

"Let me see it?"

Dave took the camera from me. "It's not a very good one," he said.

"It's worth £80-90 though. You'll get £50 for it still." Julian looked at me, noting my surprise.

"Electrical stuff is expensive over here, Kenny. You get good money for anything electrical." He turned back to Dave. "Anyway, Greedy. Even if you only get £40 for it, it's piss easy for signing three cheques!"

This was why I hated him. He asks you to put something his way. Then you do. Then all he does is haggle.

"Let's see the signatures." He took the cheques from me "Oh, they're piss easy."

"So, you'll do it then?" Julian asked,

"Make it..."

"Don't push your luck, Dave." I gave him a dirty look. Literally, as I headed for the shower.

"All right. I'll do it." he said, dumbly. Then he added "I thought you didn't have any missions lined up?"

"We found a bag in Flash and didn't tell anyone," I heard Julian tell him. "Right, I'm off then..."

"I wondered what the smell was!" I shouted from the shower.

Dave went out.

"See you later on."

"Yeah see you in a bit." Julian watched him as he went out the door, then got up.

"Leave that shower on for me."

As he came in the bathroom I went out. I towelled myself dry and put on shorts and a T-shirt, "I'm going to the shops to get Andy a birthday card. Do you want anything?"

"No," came the muffled response. "But be quick. We'll drop that bag at the launderette and get some decent breakfast. I'm starving."

By the time I had picked out a card and come back, Julian was dressed and ready to go.

I left two rolls, pizza crisps and choco Milko on Andy's bed next to his card, which I had signed, 'Happy Birthday, ARSE, nineteen again! Kenny & Julian'.

We hopped on the bike and drove to the launderette. We gave the bag to the Ninja that worked there, along with 500 drachs for a service wash. We drove back towards Eva and stopped the bike just next to Alex's bike shop. Alex waved.

"They do a good breakfast here, nice and fresh," Julian said dismounting.

I ordered bacon, egg, toast, orange juice and coffee for two.

Julian picked up his leather pouch.

"I'll give Alex some money for the Vespa."

He popped next door. Came back. Put his pouch on the table and lit a cigarette.

"What's the story with that pouch?" I asked.

"I was on Rhodes before I came here. We got it one night on a job and I just kept it."

We picked at the complimentary bread that came with every meal and dipped it into the olive oil, sipping at our water as we talked.

He continued.

"I was with a couple of mates from Manchester and a boxer from London called Bobby. He was brilliant. Every time we got into a fight with other lads, Bobby used to say, 'get your best man over'. Whack! He'd drop them. First time. One punch. It was fuckin' top! All the other lads used to shit themselves. Every time. It was so funny. No messing. He just said it every time. 'Get your best man now!' Smack!"

He laughed shaking his head at the memory.

"Then we came over here to Crete and Bobby went home. That's how we met Andy and the others. Me and my mates were going fighting with them one night. It's a good job Bobby wasn't here. We wouldn't have got the chance to start talking!"

The food came, and we stopped talking for a while to eat. It was funny. You didn't think about food much, but every time, you ate as though starving.

Just then Andy passed. Choco Milko in hand.

"Andy!" we shouted.

He stopped walking and came over to our table.

I reached out to shake his hand, "Happy birthday, Young Gun!"

"Cheers, Kenny."

"All the best, Andy." Julian put out his hand.

"Cheers, Jules."

Andy looked at our half-eaten bacon and eggs.

"Do you want something to eat, Andy?" Julian asked him.

"Nah, I've just ate dry rolls and crisps, mate. You finish your crispy bacon and soft-yolk eggs," he said sarcastically. "I'm surprised you didn't get them to cut your toast into soldiers," he went on.

Andy looked at me as I picked up a crispy piece of bacon and dipped it into an egg, the yellow yolk oozing over my plate. I picked up half a slice of hot buttered toast and put another rasher of bacon on it, folded it in half and used it to mop up the yolk. I bit into it, chewing a couple of times before picking up my fragrant coffee and slurping at it noisily.

I'm sure I could hear Andy's stomach grumbling.

He looked at me, my plate, my coffee, my half-drunk glass of fresh orange and looked at his carton of Milko.

"I'm going down the Beach road for a game of pool. Give me a fag off you, Julian?"

"Help yourself." Julian motioned to his packet. At the same time biting into his slice of toast.

"See you's later on."

"We'll be down in a bit." Julian said.

"What are you doing for your birthday, Andy?" I asked him.

"I'm seeing that bird in Hersonisos. The one that's giving me the money to get home."

"Have you booked a flight yet?" I asked.

"Not yet. I'll do it on Monday."

"Are you going to have a drink with us at Flash first, before you go through there?" Julian asked him.

"Aye. If that's alright?" He said this a bit too sarcastically. Then turned to go, "See you later on."

Julian looked after him as Andy crossed the road at Galaxy bar.

"I don't think he'll go home, you know."

"Me neither." I said.

"Do you think he's spent that money?!"

I nodded.

"Nice of him to see us alright!"

"Andy only thinks about the next drink," I said, "That's all he cares about. Drinking and shagging as many birds as he can."

"I like a drink and a bird as well, but I try to enjoy everything I do."

"I know. I've spoken to Andy about that before. I like to enjoy everything too. Drink. Food. Music. The little things. Andy just says, 'but I like shagging birds, Kenny'. As if he gets more out of it than you. So, I asked him, what about when you're not drinking or shagging? I'd hate to live like that. Not enjoying my time."

"Yeah! I think it's important to take as much as possible out of everything too. Otherwise what's the point?!"

I suppose this was another level that we connected on. Even a stupid thing like the Vespa. Andy would never drive it. He even hated the 125's, saying they whined like hairdryers.

The type of bike didn't matter to me. You couldn't see it when you were on it and the feeling was the same. I didn't care how it looked to others or what clothes anyone wore. It only mattered to me, what you were.

"That was tasty that." Julian pushed his plate to one side and lit a cigarette, "What's the 'Dodger' like?"

"Why do you ask?"

"Andy used to go on about it quite a bit, that's all. Him and all his mates from the 'Dodger' going up town."

"It's all right. It's just a local pub. I used to drink there when I was seventeen, then I went off the rails for a bit and moved away..."

"Do you live with your parents?"

"Nah, I don't speak to my dad and my mum died a few years ago."

"Yeah, mine too."

We exchanged a look, but both knew the answer.

"Cancer."

"So, after I had my bike crash and got out of hospital, I moved away and only go back to the 'Dodger' now and then when I want to feel good about myself. Usually to see Andy, although my oldest brother still drinks there. That's how I ended up over here, by chance, my brother told me Andy was coming back for a court case and I went to see him, and he persuaded me to come back with him."

We sat in silence for a few moments. "Are you ready to go?" Julian got up.

We paid for the food and drove off down the road directly opposite, which took you a quarter of the way down the Beach road. The pool room was just at the bottom, so we parked up The Vespa outside.

Andy was sitting at the bar nursing a beer. He looked fed up.

"You set the balls up and I'll get the drinks in." Julian made his way to the bar.

"Coke for me, Julian." I called to him.

"Andy?" Julian indicated.

"Aye, beer please, Jules."

"How's the ear feeling, Andy?" I asked as he came over. He picked up a cue and started to hit the white ball up and down the table.

"Sorry, Kenny," he said, hitting the white ball off my fingers as I put the balls in the triangle.

He hit the white back up the table, softly whistling to himself, and it clipped the edge of the pack on the way down.

"Sorry, Kenny."

"Right, arse!"

I placed the triangle over the balls again to reset them. Clunk. The cue ball bounced of the angle.

"Right, Andy!"

"Here, Kenny, you break." He grinned, handing me a cue and wetting the tip with his finger. He chuckled. I re-chalked my cue, broke the balls and cleared up.

"Arse!" I directed at Andy. "Next!"

Julian came over, "That was quick!"

Julian gave Andy a cigarette and lit it for him

"Who took the bandages off, Andy?" he asked.

"Me. It looked stupid. The doctors said to let the air at it. I'm getting sick of people asking what happened."

We played pool for a couple of hours. Then headed back to the apartment. We lay on our beds talking for a bit, then fell asleep. Easy life.

I awoke first, for a change. I looked over at Andy's bed. He was already gone. I got up and walked over to the balcony and looked out. The street wasn't very busy. It was hot for this time of the evening though. I leant right over the balcony edge to see the town clock.

"Julian!" I tried to wake him. "It's time for work!"

I went in for a shower and when I came out he wasn't up, but was sitting up in bed, smoking.

"It's fuckin' hot in here!" he threw back his sheet.

The apartment was much hotter than usual. I stood out on the balcony in my towel, hoping to catch some cool breeze. The breeze was warm. I went back inside and sprayed myself all over with deodorant.

"You're worse than Dave!"

"There's no cool air out there," I moaned. "It's warm".

I put on a button neck T-shirt and left all the buttons open.

Julian got up and went out onto the balcony. I followed him out. The breeze picked up. If anything, it felt warmer still.

The sky was a funny colour.

"Look at the colour of the sky over there." Julian said pointing to the horizon, "It's weird."

He turned to walk back in. I stayed outside.

"Where's Andy?" he called out to me.

"I dunno. Hersonisos?" I said, flatly.

The sky was ominous. Malevolent. A chill came over me. I shuddered involuntarily. There was a faint eerie whistle as the wind picked up. I stood there feeling alone.

Julian came out dressed and ready to go. He tapped me on the shoulder. "Let's go."

The night grew warmer and warmer. The wind fluctuated. Blowing gently then gusting and occasionally sharply picking up and dropping whilst emitting that deathly whistle.

Andy didn't show up.

I was in a mood. I was looking forward to having a drink with him for his birthday, but since he'd gotten out of hospital, I'd hardly seen him.

I just kicked my heels and drank.

The wind seemed to be carrying an awful lot of dust and grime. The short sharp gusts blew bits into your eyes and the intense, dry heat, made you catch your breath.

Maybe this was the reason the streets were quiet. The bars were still busy, but people weren't hanging around in the street like normal. They all stood indoors.

By 1 am, the wind was swirling dust up into the air like mini tornados and beginning to shake the sign on bars and hurl paper and litter up into the air. The air was hot now, uncomfortably hot. Like during the day.

Even we had to go inside at this stage.

I just stood inside the doorway leaning against the top of the bar, drinking my Metaxa. I couldn't put my finger on anything specific. I just felt low. I couldn't shake this feeling of foreboding.

Julian was standing in the middle of the bar, holding court, talking to two girls. One of them, who had her back to me, was slightly taller than him with light brown hair. The other girl was much smaller, with lovely sun- kissed brown hair, that curled in ringlets down her pretty face. She had nice soft brown eyes and a lovely sweet, full-lipped smile.

She reminded me of me. The way she was standing there. Looking like she wanted to be somewhere else. She was looking around disinterested, like when someone you can't be bothered with is talking to your mate.

I drained my glass. Looking up, I caught Julian beckoning me over. I made my way to join him.

"This is Kenny, he's Andy's pal from Scotland."

It was the same girl from Zigzag, Sharon.

I put my hands in my pockets.

"Hiya," I smiled half-heartedly.

"How is Andy?" she asked.

"He's alright."

She turned to Julian, "We're off to Krypton. See you down there. Bye Kenny," she said brightly to me.

Her pal had nearly a full bottle of beer left. She looked at me and smiled, "Do you want this?" she said politely.

I looked down at her with my hands still in my pockets. "No."

My tone of voice and attitude seemed to surprise her. She slammed her drink down on the bar and turned to leave with Sharon. As she was leaving, she shot me a quick glance. I caught her look.

Julian sidled over, smiling.

"I'm going to shag her tonight. Do you remember, Ben? The guy from London? The guy with the bleached-blond hair that used to call everyone 'geezer'?"

I nodded.

"She used to go out with him for a bit and I always wanted to shag her. Well, now he's gone home, I'm going to. She's still a bit upset. A lot of people have gone home now."

I wasn't listening to him.

"Are you coming to Krypton?"

"Nah."

"Come on. There's nothing easier than a drunk bird with a broken heart. Offer them a shoulder to cry on and you're in like Flynn!" He smiled to himself.

"Aye, I'm sure I hear Dave say that all the time."

I made sure I got the key to the apartment and declined the offer of a lift up the road, preferring to walk instead.

God knows why.

I'd never been in a sandstorm before. I put my head down against the wind, screwed my eyes shut, buttoned my T-shirt and pulled it up over my mouth and nose just so I could breathe.

I battled my way to the apartment. Whistling the theme tune to Lawrence of Arabia on the way.

I was drenched in sweat by the time I got home to Eva. It was almost as hot as during the day.

Opening the apartment door was like opening an oven door.

Fuck that. I'm not sleeping in there.

I grabbed a couple of towels, and Andy's pillows, and went out to sleep on the balcony. The stone floor was nice and cool. I stripped to my boxer shorts and stretched out on the towels. I was sheltered by the balcony wall, but the wind roared and swirled above my head. I couldn't sleep. So, I decided to relieve myself. Now to find a suitable candidate.

I don't know why, but Andy's Aunt Val popped into my head, and I popped onto the towels.

Sun 10th Sept.

"Kenny!"

I turned my head.

Julian was standing over me, "What are you doing out here?"

I got up from the towels

"The apartment was like an oven last night."

He handed me the bottle of water he was drinking from.

"Ta."

I got up and looked over the balcony. A fine layer of sand covered the streets, and me.

"Apparently that was a sandstorm from the Sahara last night. It happens every so often. That's why it was so hot," Julian informed me.

I got into the shower and washed the sand from my hair and ears. I dressed in shorts and a vest as the morning was much hotter than usual.

"We're meeting Andy in Electra for Sunday dinner," said Julian. "Are you ready?"

We used to go to Electra every Sunday as they served roast beef and Yorkshire puddings.

"What happened to Andy last night?" I asked, putting on my training shoes.

"I never asked him. He said he was with that bird. He's spent that money you know? He's got a big fuckin' bike."

"A 250?"

"Yeah." Julian grinned, "He's says he's staying a bit longer as well."

"He might as well. His luck couldn't get much worse."

Julian laughed. "Yeah, I know."

"Since he's been here," I went on, "he's had spots on his forehead, a cold sore, a wasp stung him on the balls when he was riding his bike, and when he got off the bike, he dropped it against his leg, burning it! He blames me. He says I've jinxed him."

We pulled up outside Electra on the Vespa. Andy's Guilerra was the biggest bike there.

Dave was there. Sitting opposite Andy. So, I sat down next to Andy and left room for Julian to sit next to Dave.

We ordered four roast beef dinners. Three beers and a coke. Andy had the papers.

"Here, Kenny, I got you a Daily Record." The Daily Record was a Scottish paper.

"Cheers, young gun. Where were you last night? I thought you were meeting us for a drink?"

"Mind that bird that gave me the money to get home? She's been hanging around me, I couldn't get shot of her. I wish I'd never taken the money." He looked at me catching his eye, "Well almost." He grinned "Anyway, I've spent the money." He smiled mischievously, "So, I'm staying in Malia for a bit!"

We all laughed with him.

Dave goofily. Twat.

"Don't you feel a bit guilty, Andy?" Dave asked.

We all looked at him and chorused.

"Fuck off, Dave!"

"What's that apartment block over there?" I asked. "I've never noticed it before."

"Dunno. We've never done it before." Julian answered me. It looked like a hotel block with loads of levels.

"Worth taking a look some time though? I bet there's loads of plant pots on they floors," I mused.

The waiter brought the drinks over.

We were all reading our papers and reading out aloud to each other, when, out of the corner of my eye, I noticed three girls stop at our table, as they were leaving.

It was the tall girl, Sharon, that Julian had slept with the night before, and her small cute pal and another heavier looking girl.

"Hiya, Julian!" she greeted him cheerfully.

"All right?" he barely looked up from his paper. "Hiya, Andy, how are you?" she continued.

"Hiya, Sharon, I'm fine thanks, pal."

There was an embarrassing silence.

I noticed the small girl shifting her feet uncomfortably. She could tell her pal was being blanked and didn't want to be there. She still managed to look cute though. I caught her eye slightly as I looked up to sip my coke. I didn't keep her gaze long enough to illicit a response. She was fuming.

They finally turned to leave.

"See you then?" Sharon tried brightly.

"Right," Julian mumbled.

They left.

We all burst out laughing.

"That was cruel that!"

Who else but Dave.

"Fuck off, Dave!" we chorused.

"How hot was it last night?" Dave said, changing the subject.

"I slept out on the balcony it was that hot."

"Why didn't you come to Krypton?" Julian asked me.

"I wish I had. I couldn't sleep. I had to have a wank!"

"Who over?" Dave asked me.

"Andy's aunt!" I admitted.

Julian and Dave started to laugh. Andy looked up from his paper. "Which aunt? You bastard." He feigned insult.

"Your Aunt Val."

Andy burst out laughing.

"Why are you laughing Andy? That's your aunt!" Dave asked him.

"I've had a wank over her as well!" he confessed.

We spent the whole day in Electra. Drinking beer and playing pool.

When we finally decided to leave, to go home and change for work, we got outside to find that Andy's bike had a flat tyre!

"Fuck off!" he roared. "I'll have to push it all the way to Alex's bike shop!"

Alex's bike shop was at the top of Beach road. Electra was at the bottom. "I'll walk up with you, Andy," Dave offered.

"Cheers, Dave!"

I noticed a German international football top hanging over a ground floor balcony to dry and grabbed it quickly as they stooped down to look at the flat tyre.

We climbed on our Vespa. Julian patted the side affectionately. "She's never let us down!" He smiled at Andy.

Andy glared at us and made to kick the bike, but Julian pulled away and he missed.

"See you up at the apartment!" Julian shouted.

"Aye, cheers lads!" Andy shouted after us.

Dave waved.

We were showered and dressed and lying on top of our beds when Andy and Dave came in looking shattered.

"That bike was heavy!" Dave said effeminately.

"You will get a 250, Andy." I mocked him.

"Fuck off, arse!" Andy said, pulling off his wet T-shirt and mopping his brow with it.

He grabbed a towel and strode towards the shower.

"Check that towel for spunk, Andy!" Julian called after him.

Andy opened the toilet door and popped his head out. "It fuckin' better not have!" He pulled his head back in.

"Nah, it was your pillow I used!" I shouted in at him.

"My foreskins peeling now!" came Andy's shout from the bathroom. He emerged wrapped in a towel, "You didn't spunk on this, Kenny?" he almost pleaded to me.

I shook my head at him. But turned and made a face at Julian as Andy turned to look at himself in the mirror.

"Honestly. I've had nothing but bad luck since you came, Kenny. You jinx bastard." He walked over to the dressing table in Julian's part of the room.

Dave was already there. Helping himself to a huge blob of hair wax. He worked it through his long greasy hair.

"Leave some for me, Dave!" Andy made a face behind his back.

He kept dabbing at his ear tentatively with the towel. "It isn't getting better." He seemed to say to himself.

We didn't know what to say, so, didn't say anything.

Dave took the hand towel from Andy and wiped the wax residue from his hands onto it. Nobody else said anything but he saw me give him a dirty look.

He smiled sheepishly back.

Andy picked up some aftershave and splashed some onto his hands then patted it on his face and dabbed some behind his ear,

"Only one ear to put it behind now, so I'll save on aftershave," he intoned.

We didn't laugh.

He took a cigarette from his packet.

"Can I cadge one from you, Andy?" Dave asked.

"Help yourself, Dave. I thought you would have when I was I the shower. Julian?" he offered.

"No, I'm smoking, ta." Julian seemed to be chuckling to himself.

"Can I have some of that Fahrenheit?" Dave had already picked up the bottle and was spraying it all over his body, hair and face.

I sighed.

I went to the toilet to brush my teeth. As I was coming out, Dave went in. He pulled his toothbrush from his back pocket and put a huge dollop of toothpaste on it. After he'd brushed his teeth, he lifted his top up and sprayed himself with deodorant.

Andy watched me glaring at Dave.

As Dave came out the bathroom, he pulled two sheets of toilet paper from the roll. He was just passing me on his way back to the dressing table, when I pointed at his hand and said, "Where the fuck are you going with all that?!"

Andy collapsed in hysterics.

Julian burst out laughing.

I continued to stare at Dave, deadpan.

Dave looked at Julian, Andy and finally me.

I couldn't keep a straight face any longer.

"Aah, ya bastard!" he said in his effeminate voice.

Andy and Dave came down to Flash with us that night and helped to get it busy. The free drinks helped as well.

"Since you've gone, Dave, it seems to have picked up again," I remarked.

They both left about twelve. Just as the two London girls turned up.

"Hiya," I said, "Where have you two been?"

"We woz robbed the other night," they chorused.

"You're joking?!" we chorused.

"No!" the pal said curtly.

"It's our last night tonight." Julie looked at me "Can we take your picture?"

They stepped back a little. I stood in close next to Julian and put my hand on his shoulder and smiled.

Julie pulled out an expensive silver camera from her bag. She lifted it to her face to take the picture and pressed a button. The lens extended automatically.

"Where the fuck did that come from?!" I said to Julian, through clenched teeth.

"Are you going to Krypton later?" she asked me.

"Aye." I nodded.

"See you down there then." She smiled at me hopefully. Her little face the picture of innocence.

Mine too, I hoped, as I said, "Alright."

They turned to go.

"You 'ard bastard!" Julian mocked me.

Krypton was mobbed when we got there about 3.30 am.

Andy, who was at the bar, spotted us, and made a face behind Dave's back as he danced goofily beside him.

"Beer Julian?" he asked.

Julian nodded.

"Coke for me, Andy."

"Lightweight." He turned to get the drinks.

"Your birds over there, Kenny. Julian prodded me in the ribs. "Go on, Kenny." He kept poking. "She's over there! You're dying to go over. Are you playing hard to get now?!"

"How? What happened?!" Andy asked, handing over the drinks.

Julian done his Albert Steptoe again. Sticking his tongue into his bottom lip and screwing up his eyes.

"She blew 'im out!"

I straightened my shoulders and puffed my chest out indignantly.

"No she never!" I relaxed my posture. "Aye, I suppose she did!"

Julian winked at Andy. "He's dying to go over. Look!" He went on.

I stayed at that bar for an hour! Until I couldn't hold my bladder any longer.

"I'm going for a piss."

Julian nudged Andy. "Told you, Andy. He couldn't wait to go over!"

As I came out of the toilet, I bumped into Julie at the bottom of the stairs. She smiled sweetly at me.

"I go home tomorrow." She put her arms around my neck. "I'll never see you again."

As I bent to kiss her, Julian and Andy came down the stairs. They looked at each other and raised their eyebrows. They went into the toilet shaking their heads.

I was still kissing with Julie when they came back out and made the same faces, whilst climbing back up the stairs.

We were still kissing when Dave came past and gave me a stupid, thumbs up gesture.

"I'd better go." Julie broke away "We leave early an I haven't packed yet." She stood back and took my photo again.

"Bye, Kenny."

"Bye, Julie.

Mon 11th Sept.

Julian woke me up as he entered the apartment.

"Where did you go last night?" I asked, getting up.

"I went home with that Sharon, from ZigZag."

I was getting dressed when he asked if I fancied a bike trip to Milatos.

"Aye sure. Let's go."

We drove out of Malia the other way this time. It was the first time I'd been this way before.

The road to Milatos, was about half a mile out of Malia, then turned to the left. It was a beautiful scenic coastal road.

I never ceased to be amazed at the beauty of Crete. We passed a number of the little churches. Every few miles in the remotest of places, were these idyllic littles chapels. Heavenly formed. They all had crucifixes on top that seemed to catch the sun. They always seemed framed by light. Captured in its gaze. They shone angelically.

I could understand how people could feel religious when they came upon something as pure as this. Perhaps more ethereal than religious but it was definitely something spiritual. Whatever it was, it felt good.

Perched on their own little hilltops. Perfect and pristine. With brilliant white walls. Green roofs. Gold crucifixes. The grass around them untouched. Unreal.

The roads used to twist and turn like they were tangled. Then they would straighten and reach somewhere. The churches, usually. They would burst into view. A vision of serenity.

I always wanted to stop and enter one but resisted the temptation. Feeling somehow that it would be sacrilegious. As if it would be a violation of their sanctity. Anyway, it was enough for me just to look at them and marvel at their simple perfection.

Milatos itself was nothing special. Just a quaint little fishing village. Picturesque. It consisted of a harbour wall and a few wrecked fishing boats lying upturned on the sand.

We parked the Vespa and wandered around for a while enjoying the stillness.

We sat outside the one little café drinking coffee. Everything was so peaceful looking out to sea as the sun reflected off the water.

The next few days were relaxed. I didn't see much of Andy or Julian. Julian was seeing Sharon most of the time, and Andy was in Hersonisos.

I spent my days sunbathing and walking through the old town. Enjoying the pace of life, whilst learning escape routes and apartments with easy access points.

As I hadn't seen Andy for a while, I borrowed Dave's scooter to go through to Hersonisos to look for him.

I parked the bike outside the Star bar, which was closed for the season, and walked around to the promenade and along the boardwalk. I checked the New York bar, as that was one of his favourites.

I couldn't find Andy though, and when I got back to the Star bar, the bike was gone. Thieving bastards!

So, I had to get the bus back to Malia.

That night after Flash, Julian and me went through to Hersonisos to drive around and look for Dave's stolen bike. Almost at the exact spot the bike got nicked from, we ran out of petrol!

The petrol station was closed so we had to get a taxi back to Malia.

The next day, Dave borrowed Lloyd's scooter to take me through to Hersonisos to get the Vespa. Pulling off the main street we passed a familiar balcony.

"I shagged a bird over that!"

Dave smiled, goofily.

"Nice one!" he said and pulled in at the Star bar.

When he got off and walked to get the Vespa, I pulled away on Lloyd's scooter and left him!

Later, when he got back to the apartment I was sitting on my bed, reading the papers with Andy and Julian.

Dave came in, still gasping for breath, the fuckin' actor that he was.

"That bastard left me to push the bike all the way to the garage myself!"

We all burst out laughing. Me the most.

Dave went into the toilet to wet his face.

I jumped up to the dressing table and poured all of the Fahrenheit all over me. I grabbed the Kouros bottle and did the same, just in case he decided to use that as a backup, drenching myself in it, dousing it all over my body, I pull open my boxers and pour it down my crotch just to use it up, rubbing it in and over my buttocks.

Andy was trying not to laugh. Julian was stifling his.

"What are you doing?!" Andy said.

I whispered, "When he comes out that toilet, he's going to make his way to this table and cover himself in aftershave. Not now he isn't!" I looked at the two of them and said, "From now on, when I'm on a mission, I'm not stealing any more fuckin' Fahrenheit!"

The aftershave was beginning to sting my balls. I ignored the stinging and shook the remnants out of the bottles, leaving not a drop behind. My balls were on fire now as I made my way back to my side of the apartment and lay down on my bed with a burning sensation spreading around my balls and crack of my arse.

Dave emerged from the bathroom and shifted directly towards the dressing table. He picked up the Fahrenheit, empty, then the Kouros, same.

"Isn't there any aftershave? There was loads left the other day?"

"Yeh, well, you've been here a few times since then!" I said, through the dividing doors, squinting in pain.

"I just wanted a little spray." Dave.

"Try showering!" I said.

Tue 12th Sept.

I phoned home that night and the girl I was seeing before I left was pleading with me to come home. I told her there was no chance of that.

She told me that my oldest brother, Colin, was getting engaged and that I'd miss the party.

Sorry, Col. But I know it won't last. They don't.

That night, at Flash, when Julian was inside getting the drinks and I was standing outside on the street, alone, I suddenly got a feeling of home-sickness. I don't know how or why it happened, but it did.

On the other side of the street 'Highway' was playing Deacon Blue, 'Dignity'. For some reason it reminded me of home, and my brothers. The feeling didn't last for long, but long enough.

Julian came back carrying our drinks and the feeling subsided.

"Do you fancy going to the Kalia bar tonight?" he asked me. "I'm supposed to be meeting Sharon." He winked at me. "Who knows, she might have her pals with her."

"Aye, ok."

As I was going to the Kalia bar, I didn't want to get too drunk, so I stuck to beer.

The Kalia bar was about half a mile from the junction at the top of the Beach road, heading out of town. It lies just off the road itself and if you weren't familiar with it, you wouldn't know it was there.

It's a long walk sober and a very long walk when drunk. Thankfully we had the Vespa.

The road could also be quite dangerous, depending on what state of drunkenness you were in. The main road out of town didn't have any street lamps on it so it wasn't lit up at night and the cars and bikes went screaming past at times.

The best thing about the Kalia bar though, apart from its relaxed and intimate atmosphere, was the fact that not everyone knew about its existence.

Mostly Greeks, reps and workers, no tourists. Unless picked up by a Greek, rep, or worker.

When we arrived, I was surprised at how empty it was. A few people scattered here and there. At the bar, mostly Greeks.

Sharon and her two pals from Electra, the previous Sunday, were sitting at a table with two guys I didn't know.

Julian ignored their greetings and went straight to the bar.

"Who's that with your bird, Julian?!" I poked him in the ribs.

He chose to ignore me.

"Two beers, pal." He emphasised the pal.

The owner was a manic Greek with a huge head of curly black hair. The personification of perpetual motion. He looked strung out on cocaine all the time, thus, constantly on the go, serving and collecting glasses, barely acknowledging your presence, but he served you quickly.

Julian looked for a table as far away as possible, from Sharon and her pals, which was difficult, given the confines of the bar.

We found one and sat with our backs to them.

Two female reps caught Julian's eye and he smiled at them.

"What was your girl from home asking you earlier?" he asked me.

"Trying to get me to go home."

"Are you going?"

"No chance. There's nothing for me back home."

"What about her?"

"Nah. She's just a girl I'm seeing. Not a proper girlfriend."

"Nobody else?"

"Just my brothers. I miss them."

"Yeh, I'm the same."

"I never see my dad," I said, "and since my mum died, I've been a bit lost."

"Yeh, me too." Julian continued softly, as if talking out loud for the first time. He told me how he was there at the end when his mum died, sitting there crying helplessly as his mum slipped away.

I could have cried for him. I knew that feeling of absolute loss. I knew how helpless he had felt. I knew how soured by it he felt. I know, he knew my sorrow too. It was the cruellest possible irony to cement a friendship. I had finally met a kindred spirit. Someone like-minded. Someone who knew why I felt like I did.

Felt the same despair in those last moments, when the time you dread comes to pass, clinging futilely to hope. Then the pain of loss. The feeling of desolation from which there is no relief. It hurts forever.

I told him how the priest was giving my mum the Last Rites as I knelt at the foot of her bed, and of how she gasped that horrible final sound, known as the 'Death Breath'. I told him how the priest came to place his hand piously on my head.

"Her suffering is over my son. Your sister's suffering is over."

His mistake as my mum looked so young.

"She's not my sister, she's my mum." I sobbed, and in that moment, I hated him.

"Oh, you poor boy."

Any concept I had of faith, or belief, deserted me then.

All I had, was the pain of loss.

'DON'T YOU KNOW YOU'RE LIFE ITSELF'

The girl, Sharon and her two pals approached our table.

"Do you mind if we sit with you?"

I suppose we must have looked pretty solemn.

"If you like," Julian said flatly, getting up. "Do you want another beer, Kenny?"

"Aye, please." I smiled to myself as I watched him swagger to the bar.

"How's Andy?" Sharon asked.

I looked at her close up, for the first time. She had a pretty face, and a very easy-going, disarming, manner. Always friendly, I couldn't quite place her accent, very South of England, Devon or somewhere that way.

"He's a lot better now, thanks."

"Is he still goin' home?" her other pal asked, her accent from somewhere near Liverpool.

I noticed that she had an idiosyncrasy, she curled her lip slightly, like Elvis, when she stopped talking. She wasn't bad looking, slightly plump, tarty, she was trying too hard to be demure, and not succeeding. Not my type at all.

I shot a glance at her other pal. The small pretty one. She had a lovely little face and the warmest brown eyes.

She half-smiled and took a sip at her beer, a soft brown curl fell into her eye. She didn't bother to throw her head back dramatically to remove it and at the same time catch your attention, she just carried on drinking and removed it by blowing it away gently. I was struck by her.

"I don't know," I smiled, "I think he's going to play it by ear."

The little pal choked slightly on her beer and Sharon actually laughed. Elvis curled her lip into what she probably thought was a grin, but more resembled a sneer.

"That's cruel." She curled her lip again.

I smiled as I put my beer to my lips and said.

"Don't you mean, 'Don't Be Cruel'..?"

She didn't get it.

"Whatever." She shrugged her shoulders.

Her pals got it as I curled my lips behind the neck of my beer bottle.

Julian came back from the bar with two beers and two Metaxa and cokes. He set them down, clicked his glass against mine and said.

"Let's get licked!"

Wed 13th Sept.

Andy woke me up that afternoon by banging around the apartment.

"What's up with you?!" I asked him. I sat up in bed and drank at a bottle of water on my bedside table.

"I went through to work in Aria last night and the place was fuckin' shut!"

Andy was brilliant at retelling stories. He went on.

"They owed me 4000 drachs for two days work and I only had 1000 drachs, so I went to get a bus through, but I missed my bus. So, I borrowed 500 drachs from a bird I know to get a taxi through, and the place is fuckin' shut! So, I had to borrow another 1000 drachs to get a taxi back, and then I bought cigarettes with the change, 1600 drachs for nothing!" He shook his head. "I used to earn more on my paper round when I was fifteen!"

He lit up a cigarette, and with it between his lips, he opened up a bit of paper and said to me, "Here, Kenny. You should have a read of this."

"What is it?" I sat up alertly.

He opened the sheet of paper out, still laughing with the cigarette dangling from his mouth. "A letter Dave is writing to Dom and Tim. Listen to this, 'hiya lads, hope you are both having fun in Glasgow, ha, ha, I am having a brilliant time here. I am living with Julian, Andy and Kenny now at Pension Eva. I don't work at Flash anymore'..."

"The Greek equivalent of the Environmental Health Department threatened to close them down unless they sacked me!" I shouted out from my bed.

Andy continued, "'On the women front everything is going well and I am seeing this really tasty girl just now.'" Andy paused for effect to look at me.

"I shagged her last night."

I burst out laughing.

Andy laughed also and said, "That's who I got the money from to go through to Hersonisos. She came through with me. She thinks Dave's a nice guy, but an arse!"

Andy still had his cigarette in his mouth and was chuckling so much he started to cough. "Now I see why you don't like him, Kenny. He is a fuckin' arse!"

"What else does he say?"

Andy folded the paper and started putting it back in the drawer.

"Some crap about going to London with Julian, that's it."

"Is he fuck!" Julian chipped in.

Andy picked up the empty aftershave bottles and put them in the bin. He picked up the wax tin.

"He's finished this." Three deodorants. "And these." A packet of dental floss. "And this..." Andy threw them all in the bin.

"Smelly bastard." I said.

"I don't know how he's smelly, what with all the toiletries he uses. All he's got is this!" Andy picked up a Menin speed stick deodorant. He pulled his shorts down and stuck the perfumed stick bit between the crack of his arse and wiped it. "There," he said, putting the top back on and replacing it in the drawer beside his letter home. "Now it smells like him!" he laughed with the cigarette still between his lips.

"How will he tell the difference?!" I said. The three of us laughed.

Andy sat down on his bed next to me. "Where were you last night?"

"I went to the Kalia bar. Julian was meeting that bird, Sharon."

"Were any of her pals there?" he drew on his cigarette.

"Aye, a clown called Eileen..."

"Is that the one who curls her lip like Elvis?" he interrupted me, curling his lip at the same time.

"Aye."

"She is a bit of a clown. Always trying to act sexy. Who else?"

"A cute girl called Denise."

"Is that the one from Liverpool?"

"Aye."

"She is cute."

"Yep."

"Lucky bastard," he said.

"Why?!"

"I'm going through to see about a flight home today. That's why. Honestly, since you've been here my luck's been all bad. You've jinxed me!"

"How?!" I laughed.

"First of all, I got my ear bitten off. I got spots on my forehead. My foreskin peeled. I got stung by a wasp on my balls, and when I stopped the bike to check them, the bike fell on me! Jinx! I was the main man before you came, and look at me now, earless!"

"Never mind, Andy," Julian called through from his bed, "This time next week you'll be in't 'Dodger'!"

Andy fell back down onto his bed and looked up at the ceiling. He pulled deeply on his cigarette and traced his fingers gently along the outline of his ear.

I couldn't help but feel sorry for him. His ear was now completely black and lifeless. To have any chance of saving it, he had to go home for plastic surgery.

I took another drink of water, lay back against my pillow and thought about me.

I must have drifted off to sleep, as I awoke to the noise of Andy, Julian and a visiting Dave, moving around the apartment getting ready to go out.

Andy saw I was awake, "Are you getting up? We're going for food?"

"Nah, I'll catch up with you all later."

I listened distantly as they chattered in the background as I contemplated my next actions. Finally, they were ready to leave. I barely registered their goodbyes and arrangements to meet later. I was too consumed. I heard a, "See you later," from Andy.

"In a bit," from Julian.

I couldn't quite catch what Dave was saying.

I could hear them all noisily in the stairwell as the echo reverberated and increased their volume but not their clarity. I caught "Good night," from Maria.

My heartbeat increased in anticipation. I thought of my alibi, if I needed one later, that Maria would remember they all left together but that I was still inside.

I threw back the covers and from under my mattress pulled out the German football top, donning it, I put on a black long-sleeved T-shirt over the top it, wrapped a bum bag around my waist, and put on black jogging bottoms. I silently opened the balcony door and slipped out into the warm night air saturated with that constant smell of two-stroke. And then, I closed the door quietly behind me.

I glided across the patio floor and climbed the wall and slid effortlessly down onto the pavement below. The street was sparsely populated, but I waited until it was deserted before moving quickly across the road, then darted down the alley opposite the apartment.

Several scooters were parked up. I rolled one forward off its stand and freewheeled it silently further down the alley. At a safe distance, I inserted my flick-knife into its ignition and started it. I sped off down the alley with my adrenaline starting to course through me and an internal soundtrack playing in my head.

My hair blew back with the breeze, adding to the feeling of liberation, and the sense of anticipation showing on my face.

As I approached the junction that lead to the Beach road, I didn't look up, just fired a quick glance to make sure there was no traffic but more importantly that anyone coming down the road wouldn't notice me. I sped down to the next junction and turned right, off the Beach road and headed towards the banana plantations and my destination, the German Hotel.

I stopped and parked the bike at the idyllic graveyard, aware that I was illuminated with a bright moon above me in the clear night sky. My heartbeat quickened as I ducked into the inviting darkness of the surrounding fields, careful not to expose my silhouette before I dropped down to crawl my way across.

I finally raised my head into view when I was directly opposite my intended target. Thinking, visualising my plan.

I took off my long-sleeve T-shirt and wrapped it around my waist. I began to walk quickly out from the safety of the fields, adjusting my bottoms as if I'd been urinating. I made my way to the front entrance and walked confidently through the gate. I tried to take in as much detail as possible.

The grounds of the hotel were resplendent with iridescent light, stark bright white. Tree lined paths were artificially lit with spotlights, but beyond them was darkness. You couldn't see anything but blackness. It felt otherworldly. It was still, apart from the comforting sound of the crickets, cricking in time to my heartbeat. I walked between them, loving the feeling of isolation it gave me, moving unseen through the night.

I walked into the main reception. Seeing a stairway ahead of me, I made purposefully towards it, aware from my peripheral vision of people standing in the reception area. Once out of view I raced up the remaining steps through a door and into the first-floor corridor. Rows of doors interspersed with plant pots! My pulse increased. My expectations rose. I proceeded along the corridor checking the plant pots. Bingo! I bent down to pick out a key. My heart was racing as I inserted the key in lock and heard the sweet click as it opened, and I stepped quickly inside.

Scanning the room, I saw two unpacked suitcases lying open on the two single beds. New arrivals I hoped.

People always take their best clothes on holiday. Newly bought expensive designer T-shirts, aftershaves, cameras and even jewellery. Sometimes an expensive watch for formal nights out or a cheaper daytime watch. I crossed to the dressing room table. You would be surprised but most people keep valuables in their sock drawer.

There was a large roll of notes inside, Deutschmarks, lying next to a wallet containing travellers' cheques and an Omega watch.

The next drawer contained a cheaper Seiko watch and a smaller bundle of notes, drachmas. On the top of the table was a bottle of Fahrenheit. I ignored it.

It was time to leave. I'd been in the room for less than a minute. I listened intently at the door before I prised it silently open. This was when the adrenaline kicked in. This was usually the last chance to get caught. I readied myself for confrontation and stepped out into the hall. I turned the way I had come and strolled towards the stairs. I just had time to drop the key back into the same pot when a huge muscular man approached me wearing a German International top. He was well over six feet tall. Barrel chested with a crew cut. My heart felt like it was going to explode out of my chest.

I tried to keep my composure as he neared, and I visualised myself trying to head-butt him and then escape the clutches of this big arrogant Teutonic prick. But he must have noticed me put the key in the plant pot, for as he neared me, he merely winked at me knowingly as he looked at the plant pot then back to me.

I smiled back at him and exhaled heavily. Thank fuck he didn't want to exchange pleasantries. Or comment on the football!

I bounced down the stairs and out across the reception floor without a backward glance. Once out into the security of the lit courtyard the butterflies disappeared and were replaced by feelings of elation, and ecstasy running through every fibre of my being.

The grounds were empty. I took off my German top and quickly donned my black T-shirt. Checking that no one was around I wiped my backside with it and threw it over a ground floor balcony.

I walked out of the main gate onto the badly lit road. I quickened my pace, furtively checking for cars or people before breaking out into a sprint across the fields laughing with relief and the pure joy that comes with a success. The high was intense, an overwhelming feeling of euphoria, I was alive, had a sense of purpose, I felt invincible. By the time I got back to the bike the feelings were beginning to subside as I tried to regain my composure, but I couldn't stop grinning. I turned the scooter onto the main road and twisted the throttle back to the limit, speeding, only aware of myself as I gunned the bike to its maximum, my heart began pumping again, beating through my chest in rhythm with the racing engine of the scooter whining at full revs. That internal soundtrack started up once more.

I had to slow down at the junction to the Beach road, but I didn't turn left. I shot straight over onto the Stalis road and drove to where that road meets the Malia road just out of town. I turned and drove back towards Malia, past Pension Eva and back down the alley, returning the scooter to where it had been parked. I crossed the main road and hauled myself up our apartment wall and over the balcony the same way I had exited and the part that was imperative to my plan. Not to be seen. I took out the roll of drachmas from the bum-bag before wrapping it in a towel and throwing it up onto the roof.

Slipping back inside the apartment I scanned instinctively to see if we'd been robbed. I crossed the floor to my bed and the final surge of passion subsided as I let my breath out and controlled my breathing. I sank down gratefully on my bed and lay back with my hands behind my head in triumph. So, nobody has done the German Hotel?

Fri 15th Sept.

A loud bang awoke me. I looked up to see four armed policemen bursting into our room. They were shouting at us in Greek. I looked across at Andy as he was getting out of bed.

"What the fuck...!" he started to shout.

The police pointed their guns at us. Andy stopped dead.

Our landlady Maria came and stood between us and the police. She was screaming back at them in Greek.

"What's going on, Maria?" Andy asked her.

"The police say that you have stolen a camera from a shop in Hersonisos."

We sighed in collective relief, knowing that they were here for the wrong reason. We got a little braver at that point as they searched our belongings.

"Take it easy!" Andy shouted, as they rifled his bag. They stopped and pulled out a camera.

"That's mine!" Andy grabbed it back from them. It wasn't. But we knew it didn't come from any shop in Hersonisos.

They lifted the one on our dressing table.

"And that's mine!" I took it from his hand.

"And that's fuckin' mine!" Julian snatched a camera from the copper at his dressing table.

"Have you got any ciggies, Andy?" Julian farted loudly as he passed the nearest cop.

He could be an arrogant bastard sometimes Julian, but that was one of the times you could forgive him for it. Even Maria stifled a grin. One of the youngest coppers actually smiled. Can you get arrested for farting?

"What did you say, Maria?" Julian asked, the picture of innocence.

Maria liked Julian and Andy. She always took the time to talk to them and them to her. She took great pains to explain what the police said to us and translated what we said back to the police.

"They say that a boy who lives here has stolen a camera from a shop in Hersonisos. The description does not fit any of you three." She was listening intently to the policeman who was telling her in Greek and relating it back to us in English and then our reply back to Greek for him. "A big boy, tall with long curly hair."

Fuckin' Dave!

Maria knew who they were talking about, but she didn't say anything. She actually defended us, telling them that we were the only people who lived in the apartment and that nobody fitting their description lived there.

That was it. The police left as quickly as they had arrived.

Maria stayed behind after they went.

"They mean your friend who comes here sometimes."

"I don't think it would be him, Maria," Andy told her, full of charm. "He's not like that."

Maria appeared to believe him until Andy over did it and we all started laughing when he said, "He's just a big harmless clown."

Maria frowned motherly at us, "You just be careful over here. The police will take you away to prison. No evidence. Just prison!"

That surprised us, coming from Maria, especially the 'no evidence' bit. Andy smiled at Maria as he slowly ushered her to the door and out.

"We'll talk to him, Maria, and find out what is going on. Thanks Maria. Efaristo." He played up to her.

She smiled benevolently at us all as she exited.

"Fuckin' twat!" Julian started. "Big ugly stupid fuckin' twat!" He really spat out the words.

"So, can I batter him now?" I asked, "Do I have your blessings?"

"Only if we can sink the boot in!" Andy added, slightly puzzled. "How the fuck did they trace him back to Malia? He can't be the only ugly guy on the island!"

Andy was determined to cram as much as possible into his next few days, knowing they were his last.

He came down to Flash with us and hung around drinking all night. He ended up pulling this absolutely gorgeous girl. She was blonde with huge breasts, dressed in a skin-tight pink mini dress and high heels. She had been with the little midget prick that worked next door at Georges, and he used to parade up and down the street with her on his arm, now he was besotted, but she only had eyes for Andy and the midget was fuming.

Nobody liked that little blond-haired prick, I can't even remember his name, but him and George were well suited, cos George was a little short arsed prick also. The only thing that saved George, was he was a Greek, otherwise his arrogant, posturing demeanour would have seen him battered on numerous occasions.

The little prick knew we were responsible for some of the robbing on the island and looked on us with contempt, but never had the guts to say anything directly, keeping it to snide remarks whilst hiding behind George.

He made a comment to Julian one night and I pinned him by the throat and threatened him.

George the owner of 'Georges' used to sit outside his bar, exactly like Ally did outside ours, on his motorbike, a Harley Davidson, naturally. Well that night he swaggered over, short-arsed, even in his cowboy boots. But by that time, I'd had enough of the Greeks who think they are hard men just because it's their country.

Don't get me wrong, I liked the Greek people, mostly. However, being Greek, in no way precludes you from being a dick. There is always an idiot minority.

Anyway, George tried to cut in between us by placing his hands on me and trying to pull me away.

He got the fright of his life when I let go of stumpy and grabbed him by the throat instead. I told him I didn't give a fuck about him being Greek and that I would bite his face off before anybody intervened. He got the message. So did shorty as I booted him up the arse as he slinked away with George who was equally humiliated. I wish Costas was here, I thought.

I held their gaze until they disappeared inside the bar entrance. It put me in a mood for the rest of the night. Partly because I was now expecting a comeback from them, and partly I was annoyed at myself for letting shorty off the hook so easily.

Julian left a bit earlier than usual to meet up with Sharon. He offered to stay behind but I wasn't having it.

I remembered another little Greek bastard who Julian and Andy were friendly with. He looked slightly down syndrome, he always used to greet them by punching them on the arm but as he got more familiar with them, he graduated to hitting them in the stomach or ribs. He tried it with me one night on first meeting and I caught his punch and crumpled him with a body shot to his floating rib. His face was a mixture of surprise and fear as he struggled to catch his breath.

I got to know his younger brother Dimitri. He stopped to talk to us most nights on the door of Flash and I liked him. He was scared because he was having to do his National Service. He always introduced his brother by saying, "This is my brother. He is very strong." That seemed to be the brother's cue to demonstrate his strength by punching people. I recall Dimitri's surprise the night he introduced his brother to me like this and his brother didn't try to punch me.

The only bright spot in my night was when Andy came pea-cocking up the street later with his stunner on his arm, good ear side.

I could see short-arse peering out from the sanctuary of George's doorway. George would normally be out on the street parading up and down like a little Hitler. This made me think there was trouble in store. I resolved myself to taking a beating but vowed to sink my teeth into George and stumpy and take them down with me.

I deliberately stood out on the street all night, shooting looks at their doorway letting them know I was there and easy. In something of an anti- climax at the end of the night, George and the little Nimrod came out together jumped onto his Harley and drove off the wrong way up the Beach road so as not to pass me.

When I got back to the apartment, Andy was in Julian's double bed with his girl. They were both undressed, and she was attempting to cover her modesty with the sheet. As the girl tried to pull the sheet over her body Andy pulled it away to reveal her voluptuous figure. She was a natural blonde, I saw. Her figure was impressive, very shapely, long tanned legs and amazing full breasts.

Andy was grinning like the Cheshire Cat.

Aye. You really are unlucky Andy, I thought to myself. Most guys would have gladly given their right ear to be in his position.

I went in to my side of the apartment. I could just see them, due to the fact the dividing door didn't close fully. I lay back on my bed and tried to ignore the groans.

I must have dropped off to sleep as I awoke hearing noise on the balcony. I couldn't hear Andy next door and being slightly disorientated I opened the balcony door as quietly I as I could.

There was Andy. His girl was hanging over the balcony and he was banging away at her for all he was worth from behind. Something white caught my eye in the moonlight on Andy's darkened frame.

"Andy! You're wearing my socks!"

The girl nearly fell over the balcony, as Andy turned half startled to remonstrate with me, "Right, Kenny!" he shouted "We'll discuss it in the morning! You're fuckin' unreal!"

"Arse." I muttered closing the balcony door.

Mon 18th Sept.

During the day, Andy was packing his things. We were expecting him to give us some money as he was going home. He knew we were skint as we had been paying for the apartment. Not to mention the money Julian paid out for the Vespa when he was in hospital. We knew he got £150 from a girl but he didn't use that for a flight. Two women that he met and told them what had happened paid for his ticket.

I'd even told him I was down to my last emergency English £20 note. I emphasised the point by taking it out my drawer and waving it about theatrically before placing it back. He never took the hint.

Later on, at 3 am when we were standing at the top of the Beach road saying farewell, all grievances were forgiven. We shook hands warmly.

"See you, young gun," I told him.

He turned to Julian, "Look after this arse, Jules," he said getting in his taxi. He rolled his window and was drawing on his cigarette as the taxi pulled away and I heard him mutter, "Jinx."

Something hit me as Andy's taxi faded into the night. I was on my own.

I suppose I could understand how Andy felt. Sort of. It was him after all who had persuaded me to come out there with him. Regaling me with his colourful stories. Now his part was over. Another part of mine was beginning.

I didn't feel sorry for him for very long though. When we got back to the apartment my last £20 was gone as well. Cheers young gun.

"I thought he might have given us some money, you know," said Julian, who dropped down on his bed.

I didn't say anything but was thinking the same thing. He could have dropped us something to contribute to the rent or attempt to reimburse Julian. I suppose it never crossed his mind in his last few days, before he headed back to reality.

Money never mattered to me, it was always friendship that counted. I left Julian to contemplate the complexities of friendship, slumped on his bed smoking, and went out on the balcony and climbed up to the roof. I came back inside and threw the bum-bag at him.

"What's this?!" he looked up at me, surprised. Checking the contents, a huge smile came over his face, "Fuckin' 'ell! Where did you get that?!"

"The German Hotel!"

"Eh?! When?!"

"My way of a thank you. I pay my way Julian and I always repay my debts. I appreciate all you did for me and Andy."

I recounted my exploits and spared him no detail.

We spent the next few days living the tourist life again. Eating in the best restaurants drinking nice wine with the meals. Short bike trips. There weren't as many girls coming on holiday now as the season began to wind down. Therefore, Julian was spending lots of time with Sharon and I was getting friendlier with Denise as a result. We spent most nights in the Kalia bar.

Julian had become friendly with this really obnoxious German guy called Bruno. He had an apartment behind the Kalia bar. He was a twat. I couldn't stand him. Only this time I wasn't alone in my dislike for somebody. He was squat and barrel chested and looked like the villain in Popeye, Bluto/Brutus, I think he was known by both names to begin with. Exact same physique, but quite short. Same manner. Brutish. He took a shine to Julian, always buying him drinks. My contempt for him was equalled only in his for me. He was a really disagreeable bastard. No one had any time for him, especially when he was drunk, which was all the time. I felt the same way about him sober and could sense he was going to be a problem at some point.

He was one of those strong people who want to arm wrestle you all the time. Or challenge you to lift stools with one arm. Or do coin tricks. Any show of strength.

The girls found him intimidating. Especially Denise. Probably because she was so slight, and he appeared to have an eye for her.

I hated all that machismo of being over protective towards women. Unless she was with me or in trouble, I didn't concern myself with it. And Denise wasn't with me, yet. I'd seen it backfire too many times before. Stepping in between a warring couple only for them both to turn on you.

I didn't even know if Denise liked me or not. If she did, it didn't show. I overheard her tell Sharon she thought I was arrogant. Confident I thought, in my defence. Julian liked her 'cos she could match him drink for drink', unlike me.

I found myself more and more attracted to her though. I liked the fact that she was slightly reserved. Happy to let others dominate the conversation and have the limelight and only contributing occasionally, usually to good effect.

She smiled so sweetly.

With Bruno, I always came across as the fun-spoiler, during his feats of strength.

"Ach, my friend, I am only trying to have some fun, yah?!" He spoke perfect English.

"You lot are notoriously unfunny, though, Bruno. You are trying though. So, give it a rest!"

"Come on, we have arm wrestle!"

He always grabbed you and manhandled you. Testing his power over yours and with the girls he did it to cop sly feels.

I didn't mind when he did it with Sharon, she handled him quite well.

I didn't care when he did it with Eileen. She secretly encouraged him. Laughing and not trying too hard to free herself.

I hated it when he tried it with Denise.

He sensed it. He always stopped. Just before I said anything. He knew, as I did, conflict was inevitable. He seemed to enjoy the cat and mouse of it all.

I knew he would prove to be a handful for me. He was too strong, physically.

Otherwise, I would have arm wrestled the prick and taken great delight in snapping his fuckin' arm and ripping it out of his socket. He was just daunted enough by me, to show that he was weak.

"Bruno. How many times do I have to tell you? I don't want to arm wrestle. I don't want to pick up a stool with one hand behind my back. I don't want to drink my beer in one gulp. I can't do card tricks. And can't be bothered by anyone who does. I don't want to know where the coin goes in your coin trick. I know where I want it to go though."

"Come on, 'ave another drink."

He clicked his fingers and the manic barman arrived in an instant. Super alert.

"Another round of drinks for my friends!" Bruno boomed.

The barman caught my eye, and in the only show of emotion I'd ever seen from him, he winked at me. An ally.

Even though Bruno was living at the Kalia bar and bought drinks for everyone, I got the feeling that people were just waiting for someone to start fighting with him and they would come out of the woodwork to sink the boot in. I hoped that to be true, as I had the feeling, I would be the Guinee pig to test my own theory.

The only good thing about Bruno, and I do mean the only good thing, is that he always drank himself into oblivion relatively early and once he fell asleep, usually at the table or occasionally against the bar, he needed no persuading to be helped around the corner to his apartment and put to bed. Usually by my new pal, the manic barman.

"Why do you encourage that prick?!" I asked Julian, who annoyed me by grinning, while I pointed at Bruno who was slumped in his chair at a table across from me.

"I like him, me. He's alright." He kept smiling, "You're just jealous cos he's a good arm-wrestler!"

"I don't like him!" Sharon chipped in.

"He gives me the creeps!" Denise agreed.

Eileen curled her lip, "I don't mind him either."

"Only cos he feels you up!" Julian nodded at her, "Anyway, he does buy his round, Kenny!"

He mocked me by tapping his empty bottle on the table and picked up the full one that Bruno had bought before he crashed out. I'd had enough. I made a point of offering to take Bruno to his room that night.

Once I had finally managed to guide him through the door and drop him on his bed, I had a quick look behind me to the open door, turned him over and punched him full in the face. Bruno groaned, and I left him there with his nose bleeding. Choke on it. I decided to have a quick rummage around his room.

The light came on as my hand was in his bedside drawer.

"What are you doing?!"

It was Julian.

"What happened to Bruno's nose?!"

"What do you think?!"

"Oh, he fell, did he?!"

I carried on searching.

"Have you found anything?"

"No. I just started when you came in. He must have money somewhere. He's always got bundles on him."

"Come on, let's go. Somebody might come."

I had just closed the drawer and was crossing the floor towards the door when the barman entered, to check on Bruno.

He looked and saw Bruno lying on his bed with blood on his face but didn't say anything. He just looked at us as we passed him and waited to close the door behind us.

We were working in Flash one night, when over on the street opposite us at Highway bar, I noticed a group of about eight or nine lads jostling with each other. One of them was Chinese and seemed to be the leader.

They were all doing Karate or some form of Martial art. The Chinese guy, who was the smallest of them, was kicking the canopy overhanging the bar. It was a decent height and he was reaching it easily.

The rest of the group were loud, drunk and obnoxious. One guy in particular stood out. He was the spitting image, if you'll excuse the pun, of the German footballer, Rudi Voeller. He was desperate to kick the same height as his Chinese pal but was falling well short.

He started to become aggressive and began pushing and shoving the other lads, until the Chinese guy slapped him across the face and put him in his place. He turned away and stormed past us, giving us a dirty look, presumably for observing his humiliation, ranting and raving in German, before jumping on his bike and roaring off down the road.

The rest of them jumped on their bikes and went after him. "Arses, eh?!" Julian mused.

I could see it coming, "Trouble more like."

I knew it was only a matter of time before they came to Flash. They did.

They were all standing in the reception area one night. Drinking and shouting at each other. The Chinese guy and two others left, and this seemed to be the cue for the others to start acting up. Sure enough, they are soon Karate kicking and smashing glasses.

As they were outside in the reception area, none of the staff could hear them, so it was down to us to get them to behave. In retrospect, getting a Greek member of staff would have been the sensible thing to do. I didn't.

I went down and asked them to behave.

Rudi Voeller in some vain attempt to redeem himself for being embarrassed in front of us, started acting aggressively and began shouting, he tried to push me away. I caught his outstretched arm and quickly slapped him across the face, much as I'd seen the Chinese guy do.

Same reaction. He was momentarily stunned. Then as his pals began to encircle me, he regained his composure and stepped back into his Karate stance, shook his head and in his best Bruce Lee impersonation said, "Oh, wanna fight?!" he said, putting his hands up, Kung Fu style.

I adjusted my feet into a boxing stance, springing on my toes, and put my hands up.

"Aye, I'll fuckin' fight you!"

At that moment Julian arrived with the Cavalry.

It was the only time I'd been pleased to see Costas. The second the Germans saw the Greeks, Costas, Tony and Manos, they backed off. Costas came forward and started shoving them out onto the street. They ran away and jumped on their motorbikes and roared off. Rudi Voeller looking back to give me a dirty look. I knew I hadn't seen the last of him.

I turned to Julian, "I told you they'd be trouble!"

The next time the Germans came back, Julian was away with this little blonde-bobbed Geordie girl. I can't recall her name, but she was always going on about her, 'Mozzy bites.'

I think she offered to show them to Julian one night and that was where he went.

Anyway. The Germans showed up. The same six.

This time they didn't even pretend to be here for anything other than a fight. Three of them, Rudi Voeller, and two others came at me.

I clipped one on the chin and dropped him. They were surprised. Bouncing in their Karate poses but not committing. I was up on my toes moving in and out of distance in short steps, waiting to counter them. The decked one staggered to his feet and stood behind his mates.

Rudi started pointing at me and shouting, telling me that I was wrong to start trouble with him. Interesting perspective, prick.

He was all mad eyes and mouth. I am edging ever closer to him looking to land a punch. I reached out my arms towards his face to judge the distance. I put them up submissively.

"Look," I started, "I don't want any trouble..." he stepped forward suddenly, closing the distance, still ranting.

Crack.

I head butted him. He fell back stunned. He actually looked like he was going to cry. He held his bleeding nose. It started to swell. His pals were stunned also. I shoved them.

"Come ahead!" I roared in their faces.

They must have suddenly remembered that they knew Martial Arts! Their hands went up defensively, and they started trying to kick and throw punches.

I put my hands up and easily blocked the blows. Pivoting off to the side I caught Rudi Voeller again, with a sharp jab to his nose, continuing to move in and out of distance.

He winced in pain, stood back, and in an impressive display, swung his hands in a combination, and jumped into the air, drop-kicking nothing. The three of them came at me in turns, throwing air punches in my direction but never close enough to land.

I heard the smash of glass to my right and thought instantly that they knew their Kung Fu wasn't working. I turned expecting to get hit.

To my astonishment and relief, it was Ally!

I don't know whose horse he came riding in on, but I was pleased to see him, for once.

He lunged at Rudi and his mates.

"I'll cut you!" he was shouting.

They backed off.

Ally continued to pursue them with a broken bottle jabbing it at them. He really looked like he wanted blood.

"Come on! I'll cut you!" he repeated.

The Germans turned tail and ran off, jumped on their bikes and sped away.

"Sonsabitches!" Ally called after them. He turned to me.

I was preparing myself to eat the biggest slice of humble pie. But Ally was gracious and went up in my estimation.

"Are you alright?" he asked, genuinely concerned.

"Aye, Ally, thanks."

"German scum! I hate Germans! If they come back, you tell me. I'll kill them!" He sounded convincing.

Ok, Ally.

He threw down his broken bottle, adjusted his leather jacket and swaggered into Flash.

I forgave him.

I decided never to get caught short like that again. I resolved to keep my flick-knife on me until the Germans went home.

Julian was away saying goodbye to his Geordie girl and her 'mozzy' bites when they came back. They passed just before closing time. I suspected they were waiting until I had to leave Flash. I was right.

It's a horrible feeling being on your own. When it comes right down to it you always are. I didn't agree with John Donne, 'No man is an island'. I believe that every man is an island, and that's the tragedy. Never more so when he is in trouble. Everybody turns to someone in their hour of need. And never more needed when facing the threat of violence. I felt alone now.

Julian was away, and Andy was back home. In retrospect, again. I should have gone inside for Ally, but, I didn't.

I had just left Flash. I mean, just stepped off the door, when I heard the motorbikes pull in behind me. Then I heard the shouts. I stopped and turned around.

They were striding purposefully towards me. I pulled out my knife, flicked it open and charged at them screaming,

"Come ahead!"

They stopped dead.

"Come on then!" I shouted at them.

They just stood looking at me.

I had the knife in my right hand and was beckoning them with my left.

They didn't move.

I looked around me.

The whole street had stopped dead to watch. The bars of George's and Highway were all out on the street, watching.

I saw familiar faces, workers, hang their heads not wanting to catch my eye. Still the Germans didn't move. They didn't seem to know what to do.

"Come on!" I invited them once more.

I caught a glimpse of Sharon and Denise standing in the doorway of Highway. They came over to me and started leading me away in the opposite direction. The Germans turned and got back on their motorbikes and drove away.

How much more alone did I have to be before they fancied the odds? Fuck them, I thought. The next move was going to be mine.

I told Julian what had happened and over the next couple of nights we expected them to come back, but they didn't show up. I told Julian that I would work Flash and got him to drive around looking for them and try to find where they were staying.

Julian followed them one night to Stalis. He knew a girl who lived in the apartment next to theirs. She told us they were due to leave soon.

So, on their last night, when they were out, probably looking for me, we got Dave to work Flash and we broke into their apartment.

Their bags were all packed and ready to go. I checked that they had their passports and travel tickets in them before I threw then all out the window.

We gathered them all together and made several trips back, then transported them to a building site, where we made a bonfire out of their clothes.

Julian tipped the Vespa on its side and let some petrol spill out onto the shirts, trousers and training shoes. Then we torched them. I made sure that the passports and flight tickets burned up. I spat on the face of Rudi Voeller's passport picture before throwing that on the top of the burning pyre. We stood and watched it for a bit until sure that nothing was salvageable. Then we drove back to Malia.

Sat 23rd Sept.

It was 2 am and I was sitting on the balcony listening to my tape of The Style Council, once again playing The Paris Match.

I was feeling very reflective. Things had been almost perfect, and I was in love with everything.

We were skint though.

Julian had lost our wages from Flash, 10,000 drachs. So, we were going on a 'mission' that night.

I was trying to get myself in a ruthless mood, but it was so hard because everything had been so ideal.

I had started to fall for Denise and it was hard to be hard hearted when your heart is open. I'd been seeing her home from the Kalia bar and kissing her goodnight, that was all. She might have been getting me back for my earlier ignorance, but I liked the slow romance of it all.

She was the first decent girl I'd met, and we were taking the time to get to know each other, and I liked that. It had never been like that for me before.

'WHAT A SAD DRAMA THIS IS'

It was no good, I couldn't listen to that song anymore. I was getting bluer by the minute. I put on a dark top and headed down to Krypton.

Julian was standing outside ZigZag with Sharon. I looked past them and saw Denise inside standing with two Greeks. One was Sharon's boss. The other was a barman, Stalios.

"What's up?" I asked, nearing them, sensing something was wrong.

"He's giving Denise a hard time..." Sharon started to tell me but just then Denise tried to walk away and Stalios reached at her blouse. Denise pulled away from him determinedly, but he grabbed her by the arm.

"Let go!" she yelled at him.

I made for him. Julian put his arm across my chest, "Watch it, Kenny!"

"He's a mean bastard, Stalios." Sharon tried to stop me.

As I am striding towards them, Stalios caught sight of me. He was a slimy unctuous, lecherous creep. I had only met him a couple of times, but he was always leering and fondling girls.

"Get your fuckin' hands off her!" I roared.

He let go of Denise and she came towards me to as if to stop.

"Keep walking, Denise. Go and stand behind Julian and Sharon."

"Aah, my friend, what is your problem?"

Stalios didn't come towards me. He stayed where he was.

"Keep your hands to yourself, hard-man." I stared at him.

Stalios was only with one Greek, Sharon's boss, and he looked embarrassed.

"You do not want to start trouble with me my friend." He didn't sound too sure.

"Wrong!" I made for him. He looked startled. He was weak. "You're the one who doesn't want trouble!"

I felt Julian beside me, he only came to draw me away but Stalios took a backward step.

Julian put his arm through mine and turned me around, "Come on."

I kept my eyes on Stalios, who was glad of the intervention.

Back with Denise and Sharon, "What was that about?!" I asked.

"He was trying to chat up Denise and doesn't like being turned down," Sharon told me.

"You need to watch him, Kenny." Julian began telling me, "He's an evil bastard."

"Julian, he's another one that's full of bravado. Hiding behind the fact he's Greek. I wouldn't be two minutes with him. They're all mouth and mannerisms. They can't fight because they don't have to. They rely on people backing down. I've seen it so many times now. I'm sick of hearing 'don't mess with the Greeks,' they are this and that, they'll kill you! They're fuck all!"

Denise was visibly shaken. I admired her. No fear. Just spirit. Time to open up and let me in, Denise.

"Are you alright?" I asked.

"He gives me the creeps!" she shuddered.

Even now she was defiant. She had her hands in the pockets and was striding up the street with her ripped blouse flapping.

I saw something in her that night. In her reaction. I don't know what, call it character. Behind those soft brown eyes was a soul. Silent at the right time. Opinionated when it mattered. And she fought back. I might have just found my female counterpart. A soulmate. You have to imagine yours is out there and you have to believe that they exist.

Sharon put her arms around Denise.

"You're all right, aren't you Shnoody?!"

"Shnoody?!" I repeated. "Where do you get that from?"

"I don't know." Sharon looked at me, then Denise, "She's just a little Shnoody." She smiled.

"I thought you might have meant a shoody. Like an old drunk!" I said. "A drunk?!" Julian cut in. "How do you get that?!"

"Ach, we call old drunks shoody's now. Cos of how they sing when they're drunk. Billy Connolly noticed it, "Shoody bew, aah, hawdy haw!"

They all laughed. Familiar with the Billy Connolly routine. "Oh yeh," said Sharon, "Like the pub singers!"

"Aye, that's right," I affirmed.

"What was it he said that The Old Rugged Cross stands on?!" Julian asked.

"A heew," I told him, "On a heew far away, stands an old rugged cross!" I sang.

This all seemed to ease the tension from the Stalios incident and we all sang various versions of old songs on the way to the Kalia bar. Denise did an impressive pub singer impression of Patsy Clines', 'Crazy'.

"Am a crazee, crazee for ah feeling so lonileeee!"

Man, at that moment I could have loved her.

The darkness engulfed us as we ventured out along the main road that led us out of town. Four losers. Oblivious of anything bigger than us. Impervious to it anyway.

Sun 24th Sept.

It was announced to us by Tony that this would be the last night we would be working Flash together. Only one of us would be needed now, so we would have to work alternate nights or together but share the same amount of money. A bright point though, handing out leaflets was also over.

The fact that we have been seeing girls who are friends has made us all closer.

The only dull spot being, we were skint again. We no longer heard anything about other robberies, so guessed whoever it was had gone home. None of us had anything to go home to, so we weren't in any hurry to leave. We were less inclined to risk getting caught though. So, caution became the key.

One night outside Flash, we were deciding which of us would work. Across the street opposite, just between Highway and a café, there was an opening and a set of steps that led to an apartment block. During the course of us standing there talking, we kept seeing these three young guys coming and going. They were all staggering about drunk and shouting to each other as they went from Georges' to Highway and back, then down the alleyway into their apartment. They all went down this one time but only one reappeared.

We gave it a few minutes then Julian decided to take a look.

"I'll be back in a bit. Keep a look out for their mate."

He trotted over the road, disappearing down the stairs. He was back in seconds.

"The two of them are crashed out on their beds! They've left the front door open!"

"You're kidding!"

"No. Honest. They're suitcases are half unpacked. So, I don't know if they've just got here or are leaving. But they are well out of it!"

We watched for a minute more. Then I decided to take a look.

There they were. Sprawled out, face down on their beds.

I crept in quietly and half closed the door. It creaked loudly. No response. I went in further and opened the nearest drawer to me. A watch and a camera. I put the watch on my wrist and lifted the camera out and placed it on the drawer. I pulled out a suitcase from under the bed. The buckle scraped along the floor. No response. At the back of the suitcase was a compartment containing a plastic wallet. Bingo. American express travellers' cheques, $200. The receipts inside the wallet. I stuffed them in my pocket.

Next suitcase. The same type of plastic wallet in the same type of compartment. $250 plus the receipts. Idiots.

The other suitcase was unpacked. No wallet.

I was no longer creeping about the apartment, but I was brazenly opening and closing cupboard doors and searching through drawers. They were dead to the world.

This one guy had obviously hidden his valuables. I went through all their belongings. In the wardrobes I rifled through pockets, I patted jackets. In the corner of a wardrobe was an old pair of trainers, ones that you would wear to the beach. I picked them up and tipped them back. A watch fell out and clattered to the floor. My heart sunk. No response. Stuffed into the toes, in their plastic wallet were $300 in travellers' cheques. I put the trainers back and was about to leave when I looked down at the two drunken gargoyles on the bed, their faces contorted. I saw a bump in the back pocket of one, a wallet. I pulled it out tentatively. It eased out. I opened it up and pulled out the Drachma inside, eight crisp 5000 drach notes. The other drunk didn't have anything in his back pocket, so I actually rolled him over and put my hands into his front pocket. He responded. Mumbled something, but I had already dropped the wallet on his bed and was disappearing out the door with another five, 5000 drach notes.

I left the front door wide open, as I had found it, and began to slowly climb the stairs as caution returned and I was so close to escaping. I walked down the street to my left away from the apartment and about two hundred yards down I crossed over then doubled back on myself.

Julian didn't see me approach him until I was almost at the door of Flash.

"I didn't see you come out! What took you?!" he asked, concerned.

"Cheeky bastard hid his stuff!"

"What did you get?"

"Brace yourself."

"Yeah?" he grinned.

"$750 in travellers' cheques..."

"What kind?!"

"American Express."

"That'll do nicely!"

"And 65,000 drachs!"

"Fuckin' hell!" he beamed, "We'll go shopping tomorrow at Ag Nic."

"Where?!"

"Agios Nicolas. Haven't you been?"

"Nah."

"It's beautiful. We'll hire a jeep and drive through though. It's a bit of a trek on a bike."

Mon 25th Sept.

We awoke early that morning and were whistling and singing in the shower as we dressed in our best tourist clothes. Bright T-shirts, shorts, sunglasses and bum-bags.

Julian was as good as Tim at forging signatures, and they looked easy for him. We got a taxi to the end of Stalis and worked our way back along towards Malia.

Cashing the cheques went smoothly. I never got over how easy it was. Once back at Malia we used a stolen driving license to hire the best-looking Jeep on the lot. Black with chrome alloys wheels.

Julian drove a car as expertly as he drove a bike and we were soon speeding out of town tearing our way to Ag Nic.

On the road to Ag Nic the scenery was beautiful, and as the jeep had a cassette player, we were at last able to match our feelings to a soundtrack. Julian had a best of The Doors tape with him, and I'll never forget the drive to Ag Nic as we listened to Riders on the Storm.

The road ahead climbed up to our right and built into the cliffs was a lovely white village. For some reason I likened it to Camelot. Further on, built into the mountain side, was a restaurant, perched high on the rocks overlooking the valley below.

We blew into Ag Nic to the strains of L.A Woman blasting from the stereo.

'WELL I JUST GOT INTO TOWN ABOUT AN HOUR AGO, TOOK A LOOK AROUND SEE WHICH WAY THE WIND BLOWS'

I felt on top of the world. Master of my domain.

Julian knew where he was going and drove straight to the town centre.

Agios Nicolas was constructed around a harbour. Wrapped all around it were the bars and clubs and cafes. The apartments rose away up into the surrounding hills. It was impressive. Much more high-end and expensive than Malia with a better class of shops and tourists.

The first thing we bought were new T-shirts to ditch our loud, garish tourist ones. But we threw the old ones in the back of the jeep in case we needed them again. Then we picked up some new 501's. White for me, classic for Julian. We bought new sunglasses. Julian bought a gold wrist chain, I bought a copper bangle. Julian even bought a new bottle of Fahrenheit, now that Dave had gone. New trainers and a couple of T-shirts, job done.

We sat outside a café overlooking the harbour, admiring the range of stunning boats. It was a perfect day. The sun was shining on us. We had money in our pockets. A few beers and a good friend to drink them with. If there is anything more ideal than that, I can't wait to find it.

I drove back from Ag Nic. It was good to drive a car again. "What do you drive back home, Kenny?"

"A mini."

The drive back was always quieter and more subdued. Julian played the new Van Morrison album, Avalon Sunset on the way home. Just as the Sun was setting and the sky was a full spectrum of different hues, I was lifted as I heard 'Coney Island' for the first time.

I stopped the jeep just along from the apartment, so nobody saw us.

"You handle a car a lot better than you drive a bike, I'll tell you that!" Julian said, picking up the bags from the back seat.

Tues 26th Sept.

We gave the jeep back and went to see Alex at his bike shop to re-hire the Vespa.

At the Kalia bar that night, Bruno was conspicuous by his absence. I was glad.

"Oh yeah," Julian said, "I remember him saying something about having to go to Athens. Then he sort of tapped his nose like it was a big secret."

"How do you know it wasn't another coin trick gone wrong?!"

That was the thing about being in Crete. You didn't really know anything about the people you met. You had to take them at face value. Everyone had their secrets. The ones I met were troubled in some way. Dealing with loss or family issues, or fractured relationships of some kind. Damaged in some way. The majority though, were just exploring during their gap year, enhancing their life experience then preparing to go back to a better life back home, with limitless possibilities.

We ordered a couple of pizzas and I toasted his absence. Denise and Sharon were with us. Eileen was away adding another episode to her complicated love life.

The Kalia bar could be a desperate place at that time of the morning. Full of drunks and desperados, hopefully plying girls with more alcohol. Reps pouring their hearts out about the stresses of the job.

There were a lot of heart to hearts. People revealed themselves, secure in the knowledge they would never see the person again and their truths couldn't be held against them.

Most people were unhappy about something and had come to escape the realities of life back home. It was a sad reflection to see so many young people feel the need to escape. But you can't look for happiness outside of yourself. It has to come from within. You can't rely on someone else to make you happy. Sometimes I feel sad for everyone.

Most of the workers in Malia were from reasonably well-off families and they knew this one year might have to fulfil a life-times wishes before they willingly conformed to lives of mundanity.

Some of us were there for something more than that. Hoping to find a something more that's greater than us. Just hoping to be touched a little more deeply. I know I am and that I was. I had met a friend in Julian and a Soulmate in Denise.

Then there are the perennial losers.

These are the people who go from one summer to the next. One country to another. Expecting it to be different in each place.

We are all the same the world over.

Some of those people couldn't go home again. I watched their departures, tinged with sadness. I watched them leave to catch the 'season' somewhere else. Turning their collars up against a cold wind and disappearing into a hostile night. Engulfed quickly by a malevolent darkness. Hoping against hope that something more existed. What must it be like to be one them?

Fri 29th Sept.

We were standing outside Flash about 1am when I spotted Bruno staggering down the street. He was just passing Highway on the opposite side of the street from us. He was bumping into people and just stumbling on arrogantly growling at them in German.

"I'm rolling him!" I decided.

"What?!" Julian exclaimed.

"I've had enough of that German twat. He's getting it!"

Bruno sat down at a restaurant that was closing and they moved him on. I knew he was looking for somewhere to crash out and sleep.

We had never seen him down this way before. He knew Julian worked on the Beach road, so we guessed he was looking for him.

"How are we going to do it?" Julian asked.

"We'll follow him on the bike. The minute he stops to sit down again, I'll have him." I was now well hyped up for it.

We jumped on the Vespa and followed him.

Bruno staggered on manfully. Further and further down the road, away from the busy bars. He came to a restaurant that was closed and lay down on their steps.

We waited and watched for a few moments to give him time to pass out. Most of the bars that far down were closed or closing.

I told Julian to move along just towards the banana plantations and sit there for me. I crossed the road and crept up behind Bruno. He was lying on his side, face down slightly into the steps. I pulled a wallet out of his back pocket. It was brown leather with a patchwork floral pattern on it.

"Cheers, Bruno. German shit!" I kicked him in the stomach and took off down the road and turned right. I bolted to where Julian was waiting, a little further along the road than I was expecting.

"Go!" I yelled getting on the back.

Julian pulled away calmly, "How much did you get?"

I opened he wallet. Empty.

"Go back!"

"What?!"

"Go back. There's nothing in the wallet. It must be in his bum-bag."

Julian wheeled the bike around and stopped where it was originally.

"A little nearer, Julian!" I said, sarcastically.

I crossed the road and walked up towards Bruno on the opposite side this time. A couple had stopped to ask if he was alright. Bruno lashed out at them and yelled in German.

The couple were English. "Fuck you then!" I heard the man say.

I crossed over. Bruno was still mumbling something in his drunken stupor.

"Are you alright, mate?" I asked, unclipping his bum-bag. I had to roll him over slightly to get at the buckle strap under his body.

He growled something in German and took a swing at me. He missed. I punched him right on the nose.

"You pugnacious prick!" I took off again back to Julian.

"Check that this time, Kenny, I'm not driving off again."

I opened up the bum-bag. Bruno's passport, driving license and a bank receipt for money, but no money. I pocketed his passport and driving license and tossed the bum-bag into some bushes.

I stormed back round to Bruno. Booted him in the stomach and face and grabbed him by the throat with one hand, whilst sticking my other hand into his pockets. Finally, a roll of notes. I stuffed them in my pockets.

Bruno was a pathetic mess now. Blood on his face and clothing. Blabbering incoherently. Blood and saliva coming from his mouth in tiny bubbles.

"Do you want to arm wrestle now? You little prick!" I walked back to Julian this time.

"Don't tell me you didn't get anything?!"

"No. I got it. So did he. Let's go."

We drove along past the graveyard and up on to the main road, turned right at the top and along to the Beach road and back down to Flash.

Flash was closing as we went into the toilet and entered one of the cubicles. I pulled out the wad of notes.

"Fuckin' hell!" Julian exclaimed.

It was all in 1000 Drachma notes. I began to count.

"1,2,3,4,5,6,7.....15,16,17,18,19." By the time I got to twenty we were laughing convulsively. 37,000 Drachma. Only about £150, but all in singles, it felt much more. The fact that I got to give Bruno a kicking in the process made it even sweeter.

I counted out eighteen notes and handed them to Julian, then ripped one note in half down the middle and gave him that too.

"Straight down the middle, Jules!"

He laughed. "I told you Bruno was all right!"

I rubbed my hands together, "Let's have a beer!"

I didn't know it at the time, but my night was only going to get better.

Leaving Flash on the way down to Krpyton, we met Denise and Sharon outside ZigZag. They had been celebrating Denise's twentieth birthday, after 12 am.

We bought some champagne and toasted Denise. They looked slightly bemused when I finished her toast with, "And God bless, Bruno!"

I went home with Denise that night. It was our first proper night together. Her birthday and our first anniversary.

Sun 30th Sept.

We went through to Stalis to the Beachcomber bar where Denise worked, for breakfast, and so she could collect her last wage. Sharon and Denise sat at a table, while me and Julian went to the bar to order.

I was conscious of someone staring at me from behind the bar. As the man approached us, we locked eyes and held the stare. Julian introduced me to Denise's boss, Jimmy. He had a mop of light brown-blond hair, deep tan and deep-set blue eyes, fixed on me.

"Alright, Jimmy. This is Kenny."

Jimmy continued to look at me coldly. I stared back just as cold.

"Alright, Kenny?" I detected a faint Glaswegian accent.

"Alright, Jimmy?" We didn't blink. Julian detected the tension.

"Are you the one that's seeing Denise?" he was already pouring a beer for Julian.

It sounded like an accusation. "Aye."

"Look after her. She's a nice girl."

I continued to look into his eyes searching for any sign of weakness. His eyes were so deep set and narrowed it was hard to read him. I guessed he was doing the same to me.

"I wouldn't be with her if she wasn't."

The Mexican Standoff continued. I was easy about Jimmy and Jimmy was just as easy about me.

"Can we order food, Jimmy?" Julian broke the tension.

"Aye, take a seat at the table and I'll send somebody over."

We turned away from the bar but Jimmy and me held our gaze until I was at the table and he turned away into the doorway behind the bar.

"What's his problem, Denise?" I asked.

"Jimmy knows everything that goes on. Malia is so small, and people talk."

"Just about me?"

"I know Jimmy." Julian admitted, "I did some labouring work for him. He's got a nice house up in the old town in Malia. He's ok, he just likes to know who people are and what's going on."

I didn't like being the only one on his radar.

"He's also protective of me," Denise added.

That was fair enough. I couldn't fault him for that.

The waitress came over to our table and greeted Denise warmly. She vaguely knew Julian and seemed surprised that he was still in Crete considering a lot of people had gone home.

"Is your friend Andy still here?" she asked me. I'd never met her before and was shocked that she knew me. I suppose no matter how hard you tried, you couldn't go unnoticed.

"Aye, he went home the other day to get his ear fixed."

"What a shame that was. He was a nice guy. He was a good laugh too. He didn't deserve that."

"You're right he didn't."

"I'll never forget him that night when you were fighting all those guys and they were throwing bottles at you, and Andy hit the Greek lad when he threw a bottle back! It started a riot!"

We all looked at each other. Andy threw the bottle?!

After breakfast, me and Denise went away on our own. No more awkwardness and my stand-off manner from our previous encounters had now completely disappeared, and at last forgotten.

It was as if an invisible barrier between us had melted. We chatted like we had known each other forever. We walked along to her apartment, so she could get changed for the beach. Then we sat in the Dolphin bar. I don't know what we said. It didn't matter. It just felt right.

'WE MET IN THE SUMMER AND WALKED 'TIL THE FALL, AND BREATHLESS WE TALKED IT WAS TONGUES'.

We stayed until it got dark, standing on the beach, looking out across the sea, with her arms wrapped around me.

Sun 1st Oct.

We went down to work only to find we had no job. Flash had closed. No warning. Nothing. Tony, Manos and Costa were there clearing up. They seemed genuinely sad to be leaving. They were all going home to Athens for the winter. Even Costas seemed sorry to be saying goodbye. Not me, though. I stayed cold with him to the end. I wished I had come across him in the same state as Bruno.

He seemed to grudgingly respect my honesty, as he grabbed my hand and shook it farewell.

From then on, now that Flash had closed, and our 'working' summer had come to an end. Denise and I did what everyone else seemed to do that summer. We fell in love.

I'd come here looking or hoping for something else and I'd found it. Even if it was only briefly. I'd still been touched by it.

I'd finally met someone like-minded. Even though our friendship appeared to have peaked with the summer. It would leave a lasting impression.

I'd finally felt love.

Hopefully you too will be touched by it.

Wed 25th Oct.

We moved out of Pension Eva and said our goodbyes to Maria. She was tearful as she hugged us goodbye.

We walked along the main road towards Sharon and Denise's apartment, who we were moving in with. Julian had under his arm, Jim Morrison, An American Prayer. I got a feeling of Déjà vu.

That night at 2 am me and Denise got up and went for a bike ride. It was getting colder at night, so I gave her my jacket to wear.

I drove to our secluded beach in Stalis. It looked different at night. We stood at the water's edge. Holding each other. Her feeling me. Me feeling our mortality.

I looked at her. Standing there in my oversized jacket, looking impossibly innocent. Smiling up at me. Her cute face. Dwarfed in my coat. Me dwarfed by it all.

'HEY HONEST TO GOODNESS GIRL, I'D KISS YOU WITH THE LIPS OF THE LORD'

As we turned to leave, with the only trace of us ever having been there disappearing, I looked down at our footprints vanishing in the sand.

I drove through to Hersonisos. Sensing this would be the last time. I drove past a familiar balcony. I've shagged a bird up there, I thought to myself.

I showed Denise where me and Julian had worked handing out leaflets. It all seemed so long ago.

We walked along the harbour wall and sat in one of the boats, huddled together, watching as the lights of town reflected off the water. Me reflecting on a summer gone.

This was the closest I'd come to feeling love.

We drove back to Malia, but I didn't want to go home. I turned the bike up off the main road at the church and drove through the old town. Winding through the narrow streets committing them forever to memory. I just wanted to drive nowhere forever with the girl of my dreams.

At 5 am I finally took us home to make love.

Wed 1st Nov.

Julian announced that him and Sharon were staying for the winter. But for me and Denise, it was time to go home.

We were taking the 'Magic Bus'.

"I wonder what it'll be like?" I mused to Julian.

"A bit like 'Coney Island' I expect," was his reply.

Thurs 2nd Nov.

The day we were leaving, we were standing outside the apartment. Denise and Sharon embraced tearfully.

I shook Julian's hand.

He had his Aviators on, so I couldn't see his eyes. I could only see myself.

I thought about all we had been through. It all flashed by in an instant.

Shaking hands wasn't enough. We embraced awkwardly. I stood back.

"See you, Julian."

"See you, Kenny."

Then it all dissolved.

As it was destined to do.

As we are born to be,

beautiful losers.

'THIS IS THE END, BEAUTIFUL FRIEND'.

The end...